The Readers' Advisory Guide to Teen Literature

ALA READERS' ADVISORY SERIES

THE READERS' ADVISORY GUIDE TO
TEEN LITERATURE

Angela Carstensen

ALA
Editions
CHICAGO | 2018

ANGELA CARSTENSEN has served as a school librarian since 2000. Currently, she is director of library and information services at Sacred Heart Greenwich, a private K–12 girls' school in Connecticut. She is author of *Outstanding Books for the College Bound: Titles and Programs for a New Generation* (2011), and she was the editor of *School Library Journal's* "Adult Books 4 Teens" blog. Carstensen has chaired YALSA's committees for the Michael L. Printz Award, Alex Award, and Award for Excellence in Nonfiction for Young Adults.

© 2018 by the American Library Association

Extensive effort has gone into ensuring the reliability of the information in this book; however, the publisher makes no warranty, express or implied, with respect to the material contained herein.

ISBN: 978-0-8389-1726-8 (paper)

Library of Congress Cataloging in Publication Control Number: 2018006318

Cover design by Alejandro Diaz. Composition by Dianne M. Rooney in Palatino and Univers typefaces.

♾ This paper meets the requirements of ANSI/NISO Z39.48-1992 (Permanence of Paper).

Printed in the United States of America

22 21 20 19 18   5 4 3 2 1

ALA Editions purchases fund advocacy, awareness, and accreditation programs for library professionals worldwide.

Contents

Series Introduction

Joyce Saricks and Neal Wyatt

SERIES EDITORS

In a library world in which finding answers to readers' advisory questions is often considered among our most daunting service challenges, library staff need guides that are supportive, accessible, and immediately useful. The titles in this series are designed to be just that. They help advisors become familiar with fiction genres and nonfiction subjects, especially those they don't personally read. They provide ready-made lists of "need to know" elements, such as key authors and read-alikes, as well as tips on how to keep up with trends and important new authors and titles.

Written by librarians with years of RA experience who are also enthusiasts of the genre or subject, the titles in this series of practical guides emphasize an appreciation of the topic, focusing on the elements and features fans enjoy, so advisors unfamiliar with the topics can readily appreciate why they are so popular.

Because this series values the fundamental concepts of readers' advisory work and its potential to serve readers, viewers, and listeners in whatever future space libraries inhabit, the focus of each book is on appeal and how appeal crosses genre, subject, and format, especially to include audio and video as well as graphic novels. Thus, each guide emphasizes the importance of whole collection readers' advisory and explores ways to make suggestions that include novels, nonfiction, and multimedia, as well as how to incorporate whole collection elements into displays and booklists.

Each guide includes sections designed to help librarians in their RA duties, be that daily work or occasional interactions. Topics covered in each volume include:

- The appeal of the genre or subject and information on subgenres and types so that librarians might understand the breadth and scope of the topic and how it relates to other genres and subjects. A brief history is also included to give advisors context and highlight beloved classic titles.

- Descriptions of key authors and titles with explanations of why they're important: why advisors should be familiar with them and why they should be kept in our collections. Lists of read-alikes accompany these core author and title lists, allowing advisors to move from identifying a key author to helping patrons find new authors to enjoy.

- Information on how to conduct the RA conversation so that advisors can learn the tools and skills needed to develop deeper connections between their collections and their communities of readers, listeners, and viewers.

- A crash course in the genre or subject designed to get staff up to speed. Turn to this section to get a quick overview of the genre or subject as well as a list of key authors and read-alikes.

- Resources and techniques for keeping up-to-date and understanding new developments in the genre or subject are also provided. This section will not only aid staff already familiar with the genre or subject, but will also help those not familiar learn how to become so.

- Tips for marketing collections and lists of resources and awards round out the tools staff need to be successful working with their community.

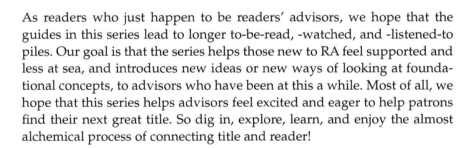

As readers who just happen to be readers' advisors, we hope that the guides in this series lead to longer to-be-read, -watched, and -listened-to piles. Our goal is that the series helps those new to RA feel supported and less at sea, and introduces new ideas or new ways of looking at foundational concepts, to advisors who have been at this a while. Most of all, we hope that this series helps advisors feel excited and eager to help patrons find their next great title. So dig in, explore, learn, and enjoy the almost alchemical process of connecting title and reader!

Acknowledgments

The invitation to write this book was one of the most exhilarating e-mails I've ever received. Writing the proposal was easy. Figuring out how to make that proposal a reality took years! First and foremost, I am grateful to Joyce Saricks and Neal Wyatt for their encouragement, spot-on critiques, and guidance throughout the process, and to Jamie Santoro at ALA Editions for shepherding this book through its final stages.

Thank you to Karyn Silverman and Carrie Shaurette for taking my invitation and running with it! Sharon Rawlins consulted on the Realistic chapter, and provided reassurance when it was sorely needed. I am very grateful.

My friends and family, and especially John, saw considerably less of me for a few years as I used evenings, weekends and vacations to work on this project. Thank you for your patience, understanding and love.

I am grateful to my colleagues at Convent of the Sacred Heart, 91st Street and Sacred Heart Greenwich for their support, and especially Head of School Joe Ciancaglini for granting me a sabbatical semester to get this book off the ground. I could never have done it without that gift of time. Thank you to Stan Burke, Laura Lutz, Susannah Goldstein and Tali Balas for being a dream team of a library department during my final years at 91st Street.

I have learned (and continue to learn) about books and reading and readers' advisory from librarian friends who share their love of books and their sharp critical minds, especially Judy Sasges, Priscille Dando, Ann Theis, Jennifer Hubert Swan, John Sexton, Karlan Sick, and so many others. I also thank my friends in the HVLA Book Club, small but mighty!

I learned to write while creating *School Library Journal's* Adult Books 4 Teens blog, and I want to thank the *SLJ* editors for their support, especially Brian Kenney for hiring me, Luann Toth for her unwavering enthusiasm, and Trevelyn Jones for being an extraordinary reviews editor. Trev would do final edits on the reviews after I (thought I had) edited them—is there a better way to learn? I thank the reviewers I worked with during those years. (I miss you!) I am grateful to Sarah Hill and Mark Flowers for the Adult Books 4 Teens column. I couldn't write this book and continue AB4T; it was a hard choice.

The generous support of publishers and the many conversations with school and library marketing associates who have become friends over the years are a highlight of this whole business. Thank you for your good humor and passion for books and readers.

As a school librarian, I practiced and honed my readers' advisory skills over years of interactions with students, and I wish I could thank each and every teen who spoke up and shared their thoughts with me, from what they appreciated to what they despised.

This book is dedicated to them.

Part
One

Readers' Advisory and Young Adult Literature

s there anything more rewarding than a smiling teen returning with a book clutched in his or her arms, asking for another one just like it? It is not an exaggeration to say that for young adults, who are in the middle of figuring out the world and their place in it, reading can be transformational. It is exciting to be part of that journey. Readers' advisory for teens is a wonderful transaction. And it can be a challenge. The heartwarming interactions may be few at the beginning, interspersed as they are with teens who want little to do with an adult's suggestions. This book combines an introduction to readers' advisory language, vocabulary, and techniques with information about what teens like to read and why, followed by an examination of the appeal lurking within each genre of young adult literature. All this is in service to the goal of using readers' advisory to help teens find the right books at the right time.

Readers' Advisory

At its simplest, readers' advisory is the art and science of helping patrons find a book to read.[1] Joyce Saricks defines advisory services for adult readers as being focused on leisure reading.[2] For teens, we need to be more flexible and include assigned reading as well. Our definition also goes beyond "a book to read" and includes audiobooks in the mix. You will see that the genre chapters encompass whole collection readers' advisory to include television and movies as well.

Readers' advisory for adult readers is in full swing. Books and articles, tweets, conference presentations, and workshops abound. But what about those for serving teens? Not as much. Don't get me wrong—public and school librarians have been performing readers' advisory with teens for years. But where is the literature about that interaction? The tweets are more about our own love of particular books, and the conference presentations are more likely to be author panels attended by the readers and fans among us. The books are mostly lists of titles by subject area or genre.

There are exceptions. First and foremost, there is Heather Booth's *Serving Teens through Readers' Advisory.* The book you hold in your hands is indebted to this predecessor. Booth leads her readers through the how and why of performing readers' advisory. This book builds on that foundation and offers an in-depth look at the appeal of each genre, through a close examination of the appeal of core titles.

This book is part of the American Library Association's Readers' Advisory Series. As such, it shares terminology with the other books in that series. In *Readers' Advisory Service in the Public Library,* Joyce Saricks defined and established readers' advisory and the elements of appeal. I establish and use related terms in this book's genre chapters, particularly tone, pacing, characterization, story/theme, and setting. And I echo the basics of genre appeal as established in *The Readers' Advisory Guide to Genre Fiction* by Saricks, and *The Readers' Advisory Guide to Nonfiction* by Neal Wyatt. These basics work very well for young adult books as well, although there are cases in which the appeal of a genre or subgenre is somewhat different for teens, and we point out those distinctions.

Young Adult Literature

Now that we've begun to define readers' advisory, we need to turn our gaze to young adult (YA) literature. The American Library Association defines young adult literature as books published for readers ages 12 through 18. (For a full overview of the changes in this definition over the decades, one cannot do better than the latest edition of Michael Cart's *Young Adult Literature: From Romance to Realism.*[3]) Young adult literature encompasses every genre and format, and it feels like there has been an explosion of publishing for this age group. Meanwhile, adults have become major purchasers of young adult literature. In 2015, Nielsen statistics showed that "80% of all the YA books that are selling are being bought by adults."[4] Obviously, some of these are being purchased by adults for young adults (i.e., parents buying for their children). But this adult audience is also alarming. Are publishers now printing books in the YA category with the goal of appealing to adults? If so, we need to be even more conscious of what appeals to our teen readers, and why.

This brings us to a brief look at crossover books; that is, titles that appeal to both young adults and to adult readers. We need to understand the appeal of YA books to the adults in our libraries who enjoy them. Perhaps this appeal stems from the fact that many of these books are quick reads, are immediately engaging, and feature good writing. For some of us adults, the appeal of teen literature may be the nostalgia factor, or the fact that many YA books waste no time to launch into the meat of the story. This isn't hard to understand. These stories harken back to a time when everything meant so much to us, when emotion ran high, when the stakes were high, when our choices were in front of us. It's thrilling, scary, and meaningful. There are also adult book groups that read YA literature. Join one and test your own theories!

When working with teen readers, we quickly learn that they do not differentiate between books published for adults and those published for young adults. A great read is a great read. Books like *Where'd You Go, Bernadette* by Maria Semple or *The Night Circus* by Erin Morgenstern are read as voraciously as the new Sarah Dessen or Cassandra Clare novel. As they grow older, teens gravitate to adult books more and more often. They become more interested in adult characters, are more aware of what their parents are reading, and are ready to push the boundaries, especially in a favorite genre. Their teachers may also be recommending what they consider modern classics, like *Americanah* by Chimamanda Ngozi Adichie or *The Underground Railroad* by Colson Whitehead.

Intended Audience

The audience for this book is librarians and library staff who serve young adults in public libraries, middle and high school libraries, and college and university libraries. This book will help readers' advisors understand what young readers appreciate about their favorite genres and will expand their knowledge of the core titles in each genre. Collection development librarians will find titles to enhance and expand their buying, and administrators will learn more about serving young adult patrons. It is my hope that adult librarians whose duties and interests have expanded from adult readers' advisory to include young adult fiction and nonfiction will find this book particularly helpful, since the genre chapters feature both popular young adult titles and adult titles with crossover appeal.

What to Expect

Readers' advisory begins with knowing our audience and knowing their literature. We look at both teen reading habits and at young adult literature, genre by genre. Teen literature can appear particularly intimidating and overwhelming to readers' advisors who are not already reading among its titles. By the end of this book, we will have established touchstone titles in every genre on which to scaffold future reading, as well as providing resources for keeping up with newer titles, and solid advice for talking to young adults about books.

The genre chapters are the heart of the book. Each chapter begins by defining the genre and pinpointing its appeal elements. Then we dig down to the subgenre level and recommend "core titles" and "next reads" to get a handle on the books to know. Each genre chapter includes whole collection advisory that highlights movie and television titles, which can help us to understand what a teen is looking for. This is followed by resources of all types to help us keep up with new and established titles in that genre.

Of course, genres blend together. There were instances where we struggled to place certain subgenres. Historical thrillers and mysteries? Historical fantasy? Paranormal suspense? To some extent, assigning a genre to a book is artificial. We thought very hard about just what draws readers to each book as we made these choices.

Again, readers' advisory is as much an art as it is a science, and every great artist needs solid technique and background knowledge. It can be a challenge to think about books for their specific appeal elements, and just why we might suggest a particular book to a patron. Hopefully, this challenge is also enjoyable! There is a certain mindset that needs to be established and practiced. When reading for advisory purposes, we keep our mind on the book, but also on the teens we know who might enjoy it. Consider *why* certain teens might enjoy a particular book. Is it because they have expressed love for another book that feels similar to this one? Tease out the source of that similarity. Is it a certain tone? Does it call up the same emotions? Suggest the book to one of those teen patrons the next time they come in, and ask for feedback. This is how we build a repertoire of titles to suggest. As we become more experienced, a well-written review can be enough to trigger a list of read-alikes in our minds.

In other words, it is important to read, especially in genres we do not usually enjoy. The Reference & User Services Association's annual Reading List[5] is a great way to keep up with adult titles and authors to know each year. The core titles in each of the genre chapters in this book are a similar resource. Many will be familiar. If we consider what appeals to *teen* readers about each of these core titles, we are on our way to thinking like readers' advisors.

NOTES

1. Heather Booth, *Serving Teens through Readers' Advisory* (Chicago: American Library Association, 2007), 19.
2. Joyce G. Saricks, *Readers' Advisory Service in the Public Library* (Chicago: American Library Association, 2005), 1.
3. Michael Cart, *Young Adult Literature: From Romance to Realism*, 3rd ed. (Chicago: American Library Association, 2016).
4. Natasha Gilmore, "Nielsen Summit Shows the Data behind the Children's Book Boom," *Publishers Weekly*, September 17, 2015, https://www.publishersweekly .com/pw/by-topic/childrens/childrens-industry-news/article/68083-nielsen -summit-shows-the-data-behind-the-children-s-book-boom.html.
5. "The Reading List," RUSA Update, https://www.rusaupdate.org/awards/ the-reading-list/.

2

Teen Reading Habits and Marketing to Teens

Do teens actually read anymore? Many librarians find that younger teens, in the seventh and eighth grades especially, still have the time and desire to read, and some read voraciously. In high school, there are enthusiastic pockets of teens who find the time to read. These are the book club members and small groups of friends who pass around the latest trilogies. But many teens let reading slide because their schedules are too full. Some of the latter will try to make up for it over the summer and during school vacations, checking out piles of books for those weeks when they have the leisure. Others will simply bemoan how much they miss reading.

For all of the reports of reading on the decline,[1] we have to realize that teenagers are reading constantly. They read on their phones and tablets, they read class assignments, they read the latest Marvel comic, or they grab an issue of *Teen Vogue* or *Car and Driver* during the last ten minutes of study hall. For all that technology distracts from reading (and it does), it also encourages it. The latest binge-worthy Netflix or Hulu series sparks interest in the book it was based on; a Harry Potter-related movie leads to whole-series rereads; and a podcast like "Serial" sends listeners to the Internet to read more about Adnan's case. Traditional reading has a lot of competition, but it also has a lot of support from a flourishing body of literature, a community of readers who rave about that literature both online and in person, and a great variety of reading experiences that are available at teens' fingertips.

Still, we need to encourage reading books for pleasure. This type of reading is important in teens' development, and it is important to the health of our society at large. There is no downside to spending time reading a book for fun. Perhaps surprisingly, teens seem to realize the importance of reading, but they often report that they have trouble finding books they enjoy.[2] As librarians, our goal is to provide teens with access to books with which they can connect and that they enjoy enough to read another and another.

To that end, we need to know the books published for teens, promote the books that teens enjoy, understand what appeals to teen readers and why, and be savvy enough to share those books with teens in ways that they respond to. We also need to defend teens' rights to read for pleasure. Teachers who assign reading over vacations and heavy reading loads over the summer need to be gently reminded of the importance of reading books based on purely personal choice. There are also many teachers who provide DEAR (Drop Everything and Read) time in their classrooms, even while the curriculum beckons.

What are the advantages of reading for pleasure? Everything from developing empathy and social skills[3] to the stress relief of escaping into a great story. Reading builds the crucial skill of reading comprehension and, along the way, improves test scores. Why is it important that students choose books for themselves? Why isn't assignment reading just as good? Being required to read a particular book, whether it turns out to be enjoyable or not, is not a stress-reliever. Choosing a book for oneself is empowering, and it helps teens to learn about themselves. Teens can choose to read about people just like them, seeking connection or affirmation. Or they can read about people living very different lives than theirs in order to expand their horizons or completely escape from their reality. And most important, reading a book of their own choice helps teens learn to love reading.[4]

Where do teens hear about books? How do they decide what to read? Teens report that they learn about books through friends and family, by browsing online, or by browsing bookstores either in person (if they are lucky enough to live near a brick-and-mortar store) or online. What draws them to a book? Cover art, movie or television tie-ins, peer excitement on social media or on sites like Wattpad and Amazon, as well as book vlogs.[5] Social media have made it easier for readers to connect with their fellow fans and to their favorite authors. Events that bring teen readers together, like teen book festivals, have cropped up around the world, some of them organized by teens themselves.

Fifty-one percent of teens believe that the best place to get book suggestions is from their librarians and teachers.[6] How can we increase this number, and how do we market to teens effectively? Many would say that connecting with teens online is the most effective way. After all, isn't that where teens spend most of their time? Admittedly, getting "follows" for a library Twitter or Instagram feed might not be easy, nor is luring traffic to a library web page. But all of these can work for libraries that put in the time and energy and find just the right tone for communicating the information their teen patrons want. Use your teen library web page to share book lists by genre and provide teens with a place to publish their book reviews online, whether within the OPAC or on a dedicated blog. Include a Twitter feed that is curated to share author tweets, marketing promotions, book award news, and new movie trailers based on favorite books. YouTube video book reviewers with popular vlogs are also a good connecting point. Promote contests like YALSA's Teens' Top Ten and promote author events.

Working with teens in person is the ideal, however. School librarians have the luxury of seeing their patrons in person on a nearly daily basis, as well as getting to know students over time, which gives them time to gain their trust. Booktalking to whole classes of students is a great way to introduce students to books that are great reads, but that takes teacher buy-in. Running a book club is a must for both public and school librarians, since these can become hubs for students who might not otherwise meet in the course of the daily grind. And book clubs are a great way to learn by listening to your teens talk with each other about books. (Read more about booktalking and book clubs in chapter 3.)

What about the teenager who is too shy to come up and speak with you? Book displays are the most old-fashioned of marketing tools, but they are also very convenient and popular. Having a new books or themed display near the reference desk or in the teen room is wonderfully convenient when a patron comes in looking for something to read. If you are stuck for a suggestion, walking to the display can help jump-start your thinking. Some librarians keep the display area nearest the desk stocked with books they've read recently, so they have suggestions close at hand. They might also include books that are getting great reviews or buzz but which they haven't had time to read yet—and then ask the teens to let them know what they think. Some teens love helping the librarian know what to give to other readers.

Displays give patrons an entry point, too. These patrons may be brave enough to ask about a book that catches their eye. Keeping these displays rotating and fresh is a great way to communicate to teens that we are likely to have the book they are looking for, and are open to helping them find it. Shelf talkers keep the great books of three to four years earlier in play. Even better, we can get our teens involved in writing shelf talkers themselves! Ownership is one of the keys to increasing circulation. Teens will drag their friends over to show off their write-up. Peer suggestions are the best. Once teens read and love a book, they are likely to tell their friends and even their teachers about it. Getting these conversations started creates momentum for moving the collection off the shelves and carts and into teens' hands.

Readers' advisory work, and the instincts about marketing that come along with it, are cumulative. The longer we do the work, the more teens will trust us, and the more comfortable we will become. As confidence builds, so will success. Also, the more we read and recommend, the more teens will share their own opinions with us. The deeper our knowledge of the books, and the more we read ourselves and converse with teens, the easier it becomes to imagine the appeal of each new book as it comes into the library. This is when readers' advisory work with teens becomes truly rewarding and fun.

NOTES

1. "Children, Teens, and Reading: A Common Sense Media Research Brief," May 12, 2014, https://www.commonsensemedia.org/research/children-teens-and-reading.
2. "Kids & Family Reading Report: Key Findings," *Scholastic,* 2016, www.scholastic.com/readingreport/key-findings.htm.
3. Susan Pinker, "Empathy by the Book: How Fiction Affects Behavior," *Wall Street Journal,* November 11, 2016, https://www.wsj.com/articles/empathy-by-the-book-how-fiction-affects-behavior-1478804590.
4. Bernice E. Cullinan, "Independent Reading and School Achievement," *School Library Media Research* 3 (November 2000), www.ala.org/aasl/sites/ala.org.aasl/files/content/aaslpubsandjournals/slr/v013/SLMR_IndependentReading_V3.pdf; "Why Is Reading for Pleasure Important?" Reading Agency blog, 2015, https://readingagency.org.uk/news/blog/why-is-reading-for-pleasure-important.html.
5. Natasha Gilmore, "Nielsen Summit Shows the Data behind the Children's Book Boom," *Publishers Weekly,* September 17, 2015, https://www.publishersweekly.com/pw/by-topic/childrens/childrens-industry-news/article/68083-nielsen-summit-shows-the-data-behind-the-children-s-book-boom.html.
6. "Kids & Family Reading Report."

3

Readers' Advisory with Teens

S uccessful readers' advisory with teens in the library begins with welcoming teens into our library spaces. Teens need to know that we are enthusiastic about helping them find the books that they will enjoy reading.

The basics of readers' advisory with teens are threefold. First, it's about getting to know teens. Second, it's about getting to know the books they read. And third, it's about knowing how to talk about books with teens. Let's unpack each of these in turn.

Interacting with Teens in the Library

First and foremost, the teens in our libraries need to know that we welcome them into the space, that we are there to serve them, and that they can trust us. How do we present ourselves as open for conversation? It can be as simple as smiling and saying hello. Keep in mind that brain research shows that teens are not yet fully able to interpret ambiguous facial expressions. If we are upset about something completely unrelated to teens, they may interpret this as anger or dislike and shy away from an interaction. If we are hard at work on a project, they may interpret our lack of a greeting or acknowledgment as indifference or lack of interest. They will rarely interrupt us.

This is challenging, because none of us has the leisure to sit around waiting for a patron to need our help. We are always working on other things. Until they get to know us, teens may be hesitant to ask for assistance. So it is necessary to get up and walk around when we can. If we always look busy, some teens will never get up the courage to approach us. Take a stroll through the stacks or head over and ask a teen if he or she needs assistance. We should make a concerted effort to smile whenever we walk out of our office (or get up from the reference desk) and into the public library space. It may seem like a small gesture, but it will make a difference. There are also less direct ways to show openness, like putting a sign on the desk saying, "I'm reading *The Winner's Curse* this week. What are you reading?" or "Ask me what I'm reading!"

Don't push if patrons seem like they'd rather browse by themselves. Once you offer assistance and they refuse, walk away. They might return eventually. More than once a teen has walked over to my desk after refusing help. Maybe they will approach the next time they visit the library.

Of course, the best strategy is to get to know the teens who regularly frequent our libraries. Find ways to interact with them on a regular basis. Create a book club or a TAG (teen advisory group), and if there is already a book group or teen advisory group in the library run by a colleague, consider a visit to it. Give the members of the group ownership of its activities. Hand over a weekly or monthly book display space, and ask the teens to figure out the display's theme or topic—listening in on those negotiations alone helps us understand what they read, what they would recommend, and why.

Book club meetings don't always have to be about one book, and even those that are can be flexible. Each group is different. Some groups manage to focus on the book under discussion for no more than ten minutes before tumbling headlong into tangents about other books or TV series or movies that are popular at the time. Roll with it! It is important to head off negative talk about homework, teachers, or stress about upcoming tests during this time, if possible. The book club is meant to be time away from those issues. Most teens will appreciate the break.

Finding a chance to booktalk to teens is invaluable. First, we get to talk about books with teens! And then there's the fact that they will forever recognize us as people who care about what they want to read, and as fellow enthusiastic readers of the books they love. Public librarians often form partnerships with local schools in order to come and promote books, along with their library's programs and services. And school librarians find this particularly valuable because it counters the idea that we are only there to help with research or curriculum-based project work. We are also there to help students find books to enjoy! And those books don't need to be literary. It is a good idea to include titles that are there for pure fun.

Getting to Know the Books

The rest of this book is about just this—getting to know the books! Chapter 4 covers staying abreast of new titles, and the genre chapters address key titles and their specific appeal factors for teen readers.

The Readers' Advisory Interview

Ideally, this interview begins with a teen approaching the librarian to ask for a book recommendation. This almost never happens. More likely, a teen will start looking at a display of books, or will roam the stacks, and it is the librarian who initiates the conversation. "Can I help you find something in particular?" "Would you like a suggestion?" Sometimes the teen will come with a friend who is already comfortable with the librarian. Most teens are somewhat shy during their first interaction with an adult, so it's important for us to be positive and interested, but not pushy. Often teens are either shy or in a hurry, on their way to somewhere else.

Still, we need to get them talking. There are two things we want to know up front. First, what is the purpose of their search for a book—is it for an assignment with particular guidelines? Or is this purely for pleasure-reading? Second, what have they enjoyed in the past, and what are they looking for now? If we can get them talking about what they have enjoyed in the past, we will get an idea of whether they are a bookworm, an occasional reader, or a reluctant reader. If they can't think of a book they've enjoyed, we might get them talking about TV or movies.

Teens who are frequent readers with a strong genre preference will probably come out with that early in the conversation, especially if they are looking for something new in that genre. Even if we can get them talking about what they have enjoyed lately (and keep in mind that this can be a TV show or movie), we need to ask what they are in the mood for at the moment. Maybe they want something different. Our job at this point is to actively listen to the teen. If the conversation stalls, we might comment on a previous book by an author that has been mentioned. In other words, we need to show that we know YA books. If not, we can let the patrons talk about books to their heart's content, time allowing.

The more they talk, the easier it is to figure out their comfort level with "content," their reading level, and their tolerance for romance. Do they roll their eyes at romance, or do they seek it out? This is crucial because romance shows up in every genre. It's always helpful to have a few sure bets in mind that avoid romance altogether. Our genre chapters will help with suggestions.

Once the teen has answered a few initial questions, we have at least a vague idea of what he or she is seeking. Now it is time to present some options. It is best to offer at least two or three possibilities, or even more. Give a quick summary of each title, and try to mention a popular read-alike if possible, to give them an idea of what to expect from the book.

These summaries are important—and challenging! When we recommend books that we love ourselves, it is very tempting to simply say just that, along with how fantastic the book is. But communicating that a book inspired one's own tears or laughter is not persuasive for teen readers. Rather, they need a quick plot summary, including words that will give them an idea of the appeal elements of a book, and why this book relates to the titles they have mentioned as recent favorites. It's important to slant the readers' advisory interaction toward appeal factors. Even without having read the book itself, it is possible to know and communicate a book's tone, setting, and subject matter by reading reviews and listening to the opinions of teens and fellow adult readers about it.

It is best to hand the book to the teen so that she can look at the cover, or the flap copy. If the teen leaves it behind, resist the urge to reshelve it right away. Sometimes readers will go back after the interview is finished and look more closely at the titles and choose one in private.

It's important for patrons to understand that this is not about pleasing their librarian. We will not be insulted or hurt if they reject our suggestions. We are happy to keep plugging away (readers' advisory is largely trial and error, after all), but we should be sure to give them an out. When a teen seems to be itching to leave, simply ask if that's enough for now and offer to leave her to look over the books she has been shown so far. Thank her, and end the interview by expressing the hope that she will come back again. Make sure she understands that if these titles don't work, she can always come back and try again. No two readers' advisory interactions will go exactly the same way. If all we manage to do is to make a teen feel heard and hand her a couple of great books, it is a good start. She now knows that we care about connecting her with books.

What about the teens we know well, who come to trust us and regularly return seeking a recommendation or wanting to tell us about their latest read? That's what we all hope for, and we learn so much from these interactions. This is where we learn about what appeals to teens and why. And this is where we can begin to experiment a bit. We all have our slam-dunk book suggestions, but what about that something just a little different which might expand their reading world in new directions? Many of us are fortunate to work with the same readers for years in a row. We can help young people to grow as readers, and share their joy at discovering new authors and genres as they mature.

Gaining trust, withholding judgment, sharing the joy and love of reading—these are the joys of readers' advisory. Teens will return again and again.

4

Getting Up to Speed and Resources for Staying Current

I t is reasonable to wonder just how to keep up with the hundreds of new books published for young adults every year. This chapter offers recommendations for keeping up, as well as lists of resources about young adult literature, crossover books, and readers' advisory.

The most important thing we can do is regularly and steadily read the books that are popular with teens. But how do we know what these are? How do we choose which books to read? There are several strategies that work. Developing a personal learning network (PLN) of avid reader-librarians on Twitter can be informative, and even a little addictive! When the same title is mentioned over and over, it's time to learn more about it. Keep an eye on the titles that make the YALSA Teens' Top Ten[1] list each year, and add a few to the TBR (to-be-read) pile. Choose one of the starred reviews in *Booklist*, or a book from its High-Demand Hot List. We might look at the most checked-out titles in our local catalog or survey the people around us, both colleagues and teens.

Most important, we need to know what our teens are interested in, and keep an eye out for those books. Our teen patrons are our best resource. Ask them what they are reading and why. Where did they hear about it? Do they enjoy the latest hot book series or trilogy, or do they wonder why everyone is so passionate about it? Lucky librarians who receive ARCs (advance reader copies) in the mail or pick them up at conferences might make them available to teens and ask them for feedback. Knowing teens' interests provides focus to our reading of reviews and blogs. And this work is cumulative. The more we do it, the more we know, and the more focus our reading takes on.

Our colleagues are our second-best resource. Many of us remember titles and authors better after having a conversation than after viewing a statistic, whether we chat by the coffee machine or enjoy a more regular monthly get-together to talk about what everyone is reading. Meetings can run the gamut from an informal lunch gathering to a planned genre study. Many of us enjoy YA literature already and don't look on this reading as a chore. But do we read within the genres that are not our personal favorites? It is important to give those genres their due, so we can truly understand what motivates our patrons to read what they read.

Keeping up with the major review journals helps us stay aware of trends. *School Library Journal* and *Booklist* are crucial, and both have websites and e-mail newsletters focused on teen books and reading. *School Library Journal* has a wider focus, including everything about serving children and teens in a school library environment, and most of what it publishes is relevant for public librarians as well. *Booklist* focuses on books and book reviews exclusively.

Reading is all well and good, but to be most effective, it is important to make notes as we are reading or soon after we finish. Write a booktalk, list read-alikes, consider subject matter and appeal elements, and consider which readers are likely to choose or enjoy this book. Is it a good choice for a reluctant reader? Why or why not? The same book will appeal to different readers for different reasons. We need to keep in mind that what appeals to *us* about a particular book may not be the same thing that appeals to a teen. It is always a good idea to listen to teens talk about books whenever possible.

Resources for Staying Current

Resources common to all genres are listed below, as are general resources on young adult literature and readers' advisory. More specific recommendations can be found in each of this book's genre chapters.

Awards and Lists

The following are awards and lists that consider all genres. Genre-specific awards and book lists are included in each appropriate genre chapter.

Amelia Bloomer Book List: https://ameliabloomer.wordpress.com/

> Notable feminist literature for readers from birth to age eighteen, administered by the Feminist Task Force of the Social Responsibilities Round Table of the American Library Association.

Michael L. Printz Award: www.ala.org/yalsa/printz

> Arguably the most prestigious award for young adult literature, given purely for literary merit.

Rainbow Book List: GLBTQ Books for Children and Teens: http://glbtrt.ala.org/rainbowbooks/rainbow-books-lists

> Books with significant and authentic GLBTQ content, administered by the Gay, Lesbian, Bisexual, and Transgender Round Table of the American Library Association.

We're the People: https://wtpsite.wordpress.com/

> An annual summer reading list of books written or illustrated by Native Americans or people of color, including characters who are people of color or Native, people with disabilities, or LGBTQ people.

Where to Find Diverse Books (from the We Need Diverse Books website): https://diversebooks.org/resources/where-to-find-diverse -books/

> A place to find even more book awards and lists.

The Young Adult Library Services Association (YALSA) is the best-known source of awards and selected lists for young adult literature.

> The entire list of YALSA awards can be found here: www.ala.org/ yalsa/booklistsawards/bookawards.
>
> Selected lists can be accessed here: www.ala.org/yalsa/book-listsawards/booklists. Many of the lists have been moved to "The Hub" blog: www.yalsa.ala.org/thehub/.

Crossover Resources

The following resources are where to find recommended adult books with teen appeal.

"Adult Books 4 Teens" column, *School Library Journal*

> This review column is a regular feature in the print journal. Past reviews are available online at https://www.slj.com/collection-development/ adult-books-for-teens/.

Alex Awards: www.ala.org/yalsa/alex-awards

> This YALSA award is a top ten list of adult books with appeal to young adults, ages 12–18. The committee also releases a nominations list.

Booklist Editors' Choice Adult Books for Young Adults

> This list is announced in December, both online and in the print issue.

Booklist reviews: https://www.booklistonline.com/

> *Booklist* adult book reviews include a note about teen appeal when relevant.

RUSA Reading List: https://www.rusaupdate.org/awards/the-reading-list/

> An annual list of the best adult title in each of eight major genres, and includes a shortlist and read-alikes. Many titles have teen appeal potential.

Databases

Novelist Plus

> Useful for finding read-alikes for a particular title, lists of books that fall within a subgenre, and genre summaries by noted readers' advisors. Available by subscription only.

OurStory: www.diversebooks.org/ourstory/

> A database of books representing diverse experiences created by We Need Diverse Books.

YALSA Teen Book Finder App and Database: http://booklists.yalsa.net/

> This free resource was created to highlight YALSA award titles, and titles included on YALSA selected lists.

Library Journals

Booklist, Horn Book, Kirkus Reviews, Publishers Weekly, School Library Journal, VOYA (Voice of Youth Advocates)

> Keeping up with reviews is crucial. The best reviews not only describe the plot, but include appeal elements and read-alikes to help place that book in your mind within the context of the readers to whom it will appeal. Also, the annual Best Books of the Year lists from each of these reviews are invaluable.

SLJ Teen

> This biweekly e-mail newsletter is a particularly good resource for young adult literature in general, specific books, issues within the field, emerging authors, and important themes.

VOYA Magazine includes a Teen Pop Culture Quiz by Erin Helmrich, which is an excellent resource for maintaining whole collection knowledge.

> http://voyamagazine.com/tags/teen-pop-culture-quiz/

Print Resources

ALA Readers' Advisory Series (this includes books on several genres).

Booth, Heather. *Serving Teens through Readers' Advisory.* Chicago: American Library Association, 2007.

Cart, Michael. *Cart's Top 200 Adult Books for Young Adults: Two Decades in Review.* Chicago: American Library Association, 2013.

———. *Young Adult Literature: From Romance to Realism.* 3rd ed. Chicago: American Library Association, 2016.

Cart, Michael, and Christine A. Jenkins. *Top 250 LGBTQ Books for Teens: Coming Out, Being Out, and the Search for Community.* Chicago: Huron Street, 2016.

Goldsmith, Francisca. *The Readers' Advisory Guide to Graphic Novels.* 2nd ed. Chicago: American Library Association, 2017.

Hubert, Jennifer. *Reading Rants: A Guide to Books That Rock!* New York: Neal-Schuman, 2007.

Moyer, Jessica, ed. *Crossover Readers' Advisory: Maximize Your Collection to Meet Reader Satisfaction.* Santa Barbara, CA: Libraries Unlimited, 2017.

Moyer, Jessica E., and Kaite Mediatore Stover. *The Readers' Advisory Handbook.* Chicago: American Library Association, 2010.

Orr, Cynthia, and Diana Tixier Herald, eds. *Genreflecting: A Guide to Popular Reading Interests.* Santa Barbara, CA: Libraries Unlimited, 2013.

Saricks, Joyce. *The Readers' Advisory Guide to Genre Fiction.* 2nd ed. Chicago: American Library Association, 2009.

———. *Readers' Advisory Service in the Public Library.* Chicago: American Library Association, 2005.

Teen Book Review Sources

Hear from teen readers themselves. (Keep in mind that your state may have a teen-selected book award.)

BFYA Teen Session

At every ALA Annual and Midwinter conference, a local group of teen readers is assembled for a live session at which they share their thoughts about the titles nominated for the BFYA (YALSA's Best Fiction for Young Adults) list. This session is live-tweeted.

SLJ Teen book reviews: www.slj.com/tag/ya-reviews/

The *School Library Journal* website includes this section of reviews written by teen reviewers.

Teen Reads: www.teenreads.com/reviews

The fifty members of the Teen Board, selected annually, review the latest books.

VOYA: http://voyamagazine.com/

Includes teen reviewers who partner with established librarian reviewers.

YALSA Teens' Top Ten: www.ala.org/yalsa/teenstopten

This is a YALSA-sponsored annual top ten list of favorite books nominated and voted on by teens.

Websites, Blogs, and Discussion Lists

Book Riot: https://bookriot.com/

This book blog covers books for teens and adults. It has a strong group of commentators, both professional and amateur, who provide essays, podcasts, lists, and book-centered quizzes. This is a great place to notice trends and keep up with hot new titles.

Disability in Kidlit: http://disabilityinkidlit.com/

Articles, reviews, interviews, and discussions focused on the portrayal of disability in middle grade and young adult literature, from the disabled perspective.

Diversity in YA: http://diversityinya.tumblr.com/

Articles, lists, and guest posts celebrating young adult books that are about characters of color, LGBT characters, or disabled characters, as well as YA authors who are of color, LGBT, or disabled. The same creators established the We Need Diverse Books campaign, which has its own site: http://weneeddiversebooks.org/.

Forever Young Adult: http://foreveryoungadult.com/about
> "A site for YA readers who are a little less Y and a little more A."

The Guardian: https://www.theguardian.com/books
> *The Guardian* has strong, sometimes controversial, book coverage.

The Hub (YALSA): www.yalsa.ala.org/thehub/
> This blog is a terrific place to find out about trends, and keep up with YALSA's selected lists.

Jen J's Booksheets: https://booksheets.wordpress.com/
> This blog is run by Jennifer Jazwinski, who creates spreadsheets tracking starred reviews throughout the year. Young adult, middle grade, and children's books only.

No Flying No Tights: https://noflyingnotights.com/
> Reviews of graphic novels for children and teens. It includes an invaluable Teen Title Core List: http://noflyingnotights.com/blog/2017/06/16/teen-title-core-list/.

Reading Rants: www.readingrants.org/
> Jennifer Hubert Swan was one of the first YA literature blogger reviewers and continues to be one of the best. She mixes in adult titles with teen appeal, and ends the year with a Best list.

Teen Librarian Toolbox: www.teenlibrariantoolbox.com/
> This *School Library Journal* blog is full of book reviews and lists, which are particularly strong in realistic fiction.

Additional Sources

Entertainment Weekly and *People Magazine*
> A review in the book sections of either of these publications is an indication of likely break-out popularity with the general public. *Entertainment Weekly* is also a great way to stay abreast of relevant movie and television shows, both popular current shows and deals around upcoming shows based on books.

Edelweiss and NetGalley

For access to advanced e-galleys, sign up and identify yourself as a librarian. The thrill of being one of the first to read a new title may motivate you, and some teens will be impressed.

Library Reads and IndieNext

These monthly lists of recommended upcoming titles (created by librarians and booksellers, respectively) focus on adult books, many of which have crossover appeal. They also include the occasional young adult title.

Publisher Marketing Newsletters

Most publishers offer a monthly e-mail newsletter, which will keep you up-to-date on new and upcoming titles, conference events, and giveaways.

Twitter

Beyond developing a personal learning network on Twitter (i.e., following fellow librarians, authors, and publishers you enjoy and learn from), there are also recommended hashtags that will clue you in to conversations and individual tweets about books, among them:

- #ewgcya (Early Word Galley Chat—librarians chatting about books pre-publication)
- #readadv (readers' advisory librarians add this hashtag to their tweets when relevant)
- #kidlit or #YAlit (tweets about children's and teen books sometimes include this hashtag)

NOTE

1. For more information, see www.ala.org/yalsa/teenstopten.

5

How This Book Works

The genre chapters are the heart of this book. They are intended as a launching point for learning about each genre, and they follow a common template. Each begins with a definition of the genre and an explanation of its appeal for young adults, elucidating what teen fans love about the genre.

Then each genre is broken down into key subgenres. The subgenre categories are sometimes standard to publishing and librarianship, and sometimes more creative. The creative categories grow out of thinking through how teen readers experience the books within these genres and what exactly appeals most to them. For example, in the "Nonfiction" chapter, the categories are a mixture of type of reading experience, subject area, and the purpose of the book.

Each subgenre is defined and explicated with four book titles—one Core Title and three Next Reads. Each of these is annotated, and these annotations focus on the appeal factors for that book, as an exemplar of what appeals to teens about books in that subgenre. Core Titles provide both a starting place for readers new to young adult literature, and ways for experienced young adult librarians to think about the appeal of each title. They are meant to help us think about how to articulate that appeal within our work as readers' advisors. The Next Reads do the same, showing other angles of the appeal of the subgenre.

Within each subgenre, every effort has been made to include one adult title with teen appeal, and it is usually the last of the four. There are two reasons for this. First, teens don't discriminate. A great read is a great read, no matter which audience it was originally published for, and there are iconic adult titles in every genre. Second, one of the audiences for whom this book was conceived is librarians who focus on serving adults, but who often end up helping teens as well. We hope that the adult titles mentioned here will provide the basis of a scaffolded knowledge of teen literature and its appeal.

Choosing these subgenres and titles was challenging, and these chapters are hardly exhaustive. Many books (and many much-loved authors) were left on the cutting-room floor as we worked to focus in on the articulation of appeal without overwhelming the reader with lists of books. We hope that this scaffold provides the tools needed to identify the categories into which new titles might fall, more easily see those elements within each new book that lend it appeal, and imagine how to promote and suggest these elements to the books' ideal readers.

The treatments of the various subgenres, with their Core Title and Next Reads recommendations, are followed by a Whole Collection listing of television and movie titles in the genre, specific advice about providing readers' advisory to the genre's fans, and resources particular to the genre. These resources are meant to help with orientation to the genre and keeping up with new trends and titles. They include books, journals, websites, blogs, awards, and more. (More general resources for staying current have already been provided in chapter 4.)

Graphic novel recommendations are included within each genre, not separated out. They are considered a format, not a genre. Audiobooks are mentioned within Core Title and Next Read annotations. You might also notice that only the first book in a series or trilogy is mentioned. There are plenty of places to find the titles of the complete series.

Young adult books with particular appeal for adult readers are designated with a star (★).

Core and Next Read titles are followed, where applicable, by a list of the awards each has won and any best list or award list to which it has been named. For example:

> *Gabi, a Girl in Pieces,* by Isabel Quintero (Morris Award, BFYA, AAYA, QP Top Ten, Américas Honor 2015)

Here are the abbreviations you need to know:

AAYA: Amazing Audiobooks for Young Adults (YALSA)

AAYA Top Ten

Alex: Alex Awards are given to ten adult books with appeal to young adults (YALSA)

Américas: Book award for portrayal of Latin America, the Caribbean, or Latinos in the United States

BBYA: Best Books for Young Adults (before 2011), for quality and appeal (YALSA)

BBYA Top Ten

BFYA: Best Fiction for Young Adults (after 2010), for quality and appeal (YALSA)

BFYA Top Ten

Edgar: The Edgar Awards given by the Mystery Writers of America

GGNT: Great Graphic Novels for Teens

GGNT Top Ten

Horn Book Award: Boston Globe/Horn Book Award

Horn Book Honor: Boston Globe/Horn Book Honor

Morris Award: William C. Morris YA Debut Award, sponsored by YALSA

Morris Finalist: William C. Morris YA Debut Award, shortlist

NBA: National Book Award

O'Dell: Scott O'Dell Award for Historical Fiction

Odyssey Award: YALSA and ALSC joint award for best audiobook

Odyssey Honor: YALSA and ALSC joint award for best audiobook

PPYA: Popular Paperbacks for Young Adults (YALSA, indicates longevity of appeal)

Printz Award: Michael L. Printz Award for literary merit (YALSA)

Printz Honor: Michael L. Printz honor book (YALSA)

QP: Quick Picks for Reluctant Young Adult Readers (YALSA)

QP Top Ten

Sydney Taylor: Sydney Taylor Book Award, for books that portray the Jewish experience

TTT: Teens' Top Ten, voted by teens (YALSA)

YALSA Nonfiction Award: YALSA Award for Excellence in Nonfiction winner

YALSA Nonfiction Finalist: YALSA Award for Excellence in Nonfiction, shortlist

Part Two

6

Realistic Fiction

Realistic fiction reflects everyday life. For teens, that means friends, family, school, romantic relationships, and extracurricular pursuits like music, drama, sports, and jobs. Realistic young adult literature runs the gamut from teens' typical experiences to teens living on the edge, fighting to survive poverty, abuse, bullying, or mental or physical illness. Issues with which society at large is struggling are reflected in books for a teen audience, whether immigration, racial prejudice and discrimination, or sexual identity.

At the root of realistic fiction are the themes of self-discovery, coming of age, and forging one's own identity. Often protagonists are transformed by the events of the plot, which either change the protagonists' direction or clarify what is important to them. Alongside identity, realistic fiction may address the meaning of life, personal priorities, and overcoming the roadblocks to fulfilling goals. Realistic fiction encompasses all kinds of experiences, good and bad, funny and tragic, poetic and crass, romantic and violent.

As one might imagine, realistic fiction ranges widely from books about friendship and love to books about suicide or drug abuse. In recent years, the envelope of what is considered appropriate for teens has been pushed again and again, with librarians often defending the rights of teens to read about intense and edgy themes in books that are challenged in school and public library collections. Sexuality is addressed more openly and positively every year. Both heterosexual and homosexual teenaged protagonists engage in healthy romantic relationships. LGBTQ characters are increasingly common, and are often portrayed in a positive and loving light.

More and more titles incorporating diversity of all types are being published for the YA audience, thanks to the Diversity in YA, We Need Diverse Books, and OwnVoices movements. Skin color, race, and ethnicity are common themes, yes, but religion, culture, socioeconomic status, gender, ability, sexual identity, and geography are also addressed in teen books.

Before moving on to appeal, it is necessary to address one thorny question. Is a book set in what might be considered the recent past, such as the 1980s, realistic fiction, or is it historical fiction? The answer lies in appeal. The primary appeal of, for example, *Eleanor & Park* is the love story, the central relationship and its obstacles. This book is popular with the same readers who read Nicola Yoon and John Green and for many of the same reasons. Therefore, *Eleanor & Park* is considered by most to be a realistic read. But a book like *The Smell of Other People's Houses* by Bonnie-Sue Hitchcock, which is set only a decade earlier, does feel more distant in time and unfamiliar in setting. The answer is to talk over the book with readers. Introduce the subject matter and mention the time period. And then let them decide.

Realistic fiction forms the backbone of YA literature. It is the most heavily published and award-winning genre, and it is largely what the general public thinks of when the topic of YA literature comes up (along with dystopian hits like *Divergent* and *The Hunger Games*). It is also the most popular genre with the majority of teens.

Appeal

Teens are drawn to realistic fiction because it is familiar. It can be reassuring to read about people just like them, who have similar interests or are facing a similar situation. Teens seek protagonists who are identifiable, whether it is an excellent student who is feeling pressured by driven parents, or a good kid who is struggling to help his parents make ends meet. The recognizable is comforting for those who feel isolated or alone with the intensity of their experiences and feelings. And sometimes a reader finds a good cry comforting and chooses a weeper like *The Names They Gave Us* by Emery Lord.

Teens are also drawn to realistic fiction because it provides a window into lives that are different from their own. Realistic fiction can illuminate a culture within their own country, as in S.K. Ali's *Saints and Misfits,* or it can introduce them to ways of life on other continents. Books like *If I Was Your Girl* and *The Great American Whatever* are great stories, but they also provide windows and mirrors that help build empathy for and understanding of LGBTQ youth. A book like *Tash Hearts Tolstoy* provides a clear understanding of asexuality.

Teens are often confronted with situations for the first time and don't know who to turn to for advice. Maybe they need to stand up for themselves, like Jade in *Piecing Me Together*. Maybe they are grieving, like Matt in *The Boy in the Black Suit*. Maybe they are curious about mental illness or drug addiction, or they want to understand what a friend is going through. A book like *Recovery Road* by Blake Nelson might be just what they are looking for.

And don't forget: realistic fiction can be purely entertaining. Many of the books that include heavy topics do so with levity and love. Some provide a few hours of pure escape, perhaps to Italy with Lina in *Love & Gelato*. It is impossible to generalize. But it is fair to say that the decision of which realistic novel a teen will pick up next largely rests on its characters, tone, and subject matter.

Characterization

An authentic teen protagonist is all-important. Voice is everything. Part of that is tone, and part of it is character. Some readers want to get inside the head of the protagonist, which is why first-person narratives are so popular. Consider E. R. Frank's *Dime*. Knowing Dime's dreams and aspirations, recognizing her inner sweetness, helps the reader to weather her terrible story. Other readers prefer a third-person narration that leaves more to the imagination, one that keeps them guessing about the protagonist's motivation. Either way, it is crucial that a teen character's experiences ring true and that characters are transformed by those experiences. And if a teen does not talk like a teen, no reader is going to buy it (literally or figuratively).

Tone

Tone or atmosphere is about the "feel" of a book. Realistic fiction encompasses every imaginable tone, so it is important to get to the bottom of what a particular reader is seeking. Tone ranges from frivolous to bleak, from antagonistic to romantic, from serious to satirical. Does the reader seek a light romp or a dark, dramatic story? The days when YA books could be depended on for a happy ending are past, so it is important to find out just how dark a reader is willing to go.

Story/Theme

Does the reader enjoy issue-oriented, emotional, or plot-oriented stories? All of these and myriad combinations are available. Plot itself can take a back seat to coming-of-age themes, relationship dramas, or identity nuances. There are two popular narrative techniques that need to be vetted. Alternating multiple points of view is hugely popular with some readers (fans of Jodi Picoult, for example) and loathed by others. Similarly, does the narrative need to be chronological? Teens' tolerance for an inventive use of flashbacks (think *If I Stay* by Gayle Forman) varies drastically.

Setting

Setting also runs the gamut—from urban to rural, suburban, small town, inside the United States, or in another country. Is the reader interested in contrasts of wealth and poverty? A place familiar to them or somewhere new? Common tropes include the road trip, boarding school, summer beach vacation, or European travel. Again, tone is key. If a teen is interested in a story set in a boarding school, there are many options, from the clever (*The Disreputable History of Frankie Landau-Banks* by E. Lockhart) to the tragic (*And We Stay* by Jenny Hubbard).

Pacing

In the genre of realistic fiction, a slower pace is sought out by some readers. They enjoy authors who take their time establishing relationships in order to increase a story's impact. Sarah Dessen is a good example, and her readers love her for it. At the other end of the spectrum are snappy books in which witty dialogue propels the pace forward. This is a good bet for the teen who seeks a book that reads quickly, with short chapters, and perhaps alternating narrators telling different sides of the story. Of course, some realistic fiction is page-turning because the reader needs to know what happens to a compelling character.

Key Subgenres and Core Titles in Realistic Fiction
Coming-of-Age Books Emphasizing Friends and Family

We begin with books about teens whose lives are full of family, friends, school, and activities. They fit in or don't, they find themselves, dream of the perfect relationship, fall in and out of love, live through self-doubt and insecurity, are moody and changeable, listen to music, play sports, rebel against their parents, dream of escaping their hometowns, and head off to college or not. They navigate growing pains, and figure out who they are and what they want from life. These books allow teens to see themselves in fiction and understand what the people around them are experiencing, too.

CORE TITLE

Gabi, a Girl in Pieces, by Isabel Quintero (Morris Award, BFYA, AAYA Top Ten, QP Top Ten, Américas Honor 2015)

Gabi is a Mexican American high school student living in Berkeley, California. This novel is her senior year journal, and consists of both text and the occasional illustration. Gabi loves writing and reading poetry, she loves her friends, and she loves food. She struggles with issues like body image, being a "good girl" while staying true to herself, her mother's double standards, her ethnicity, and her homeless father's drug addiction. Her best friend Sebastian is kicked out of the house when he comes out to his parents, another friend becomes pregnant after being raped, and another has an abortion because her religious parents would kill her if they found out she was pregnant. Gabi supports her friends through their tribulations even while bravely taking charge of her own life, becoming involved with her first boyfriend and applying to college (while her mother accuses her of trying to be white). There is a surfeit of issues in this novel, but it is full of life and love, and it has a perfectly voiced Latina teen who is a fully formed, uncliched, independent wonder with whom many teenagers will identify.

NEXT READS

The Summer I Turned Pretty, by Jenny Han (BBYA 2010)

Every summer Isabella (Belly), her mother, and her brother Steven join Susannah and her two sons at their beach house. Belly has always wanted to be included in the boys' activities, and she has always had a crush on Susannah's older son, Conrad. This summer she is on the cusp of turning sixteen and the dynamics are shifting. Conrad's younger brother Jeremiah forms a crush on her, but she starts dating nice guy Cam, her first boyfriend, until their romance peters out. And unbeknownst to any of them, Susannah is ill with cancer. This first novel in a trilogy balances the playful ease of summer with the moodiness of growing and changing teenagers, and finds poignancy and depth in authentic characters and flashbacks. Belly's realistic first-person narrative voice anchors this great choice for readers who are seeking a breezy summer beach experience that is much more than fluff. This book is a favorite of younger teens.

★*The Serpent King,* by Jeff Zentner (Morris Award, BFYA Top Ten, QP 2017)

In alternating chapters, readers come to know three misfit best friends living in rural Tennessee. Lydia has supportive parents and a popular fashion blog that she hopes will get her into New York University. Dillard is the son of a snake-handling preacher imprisoned for possession of child pornography. His parents expect Dill to quit high school and work to support the family. Travis escapes into a fantasy book series and works at the lumber yard, while trying to survive an abusive father. Dill can't bring himself to admit to Lydia that he's in love with her, and Lydia can't stand that Dill is planning to give in to his parents' wishes rather than pursue his talent as a singer/songwriter. Then tragedy strikes. This deeply emotional, character-centered book with a strong rural setting is about self-preservation and supporting your friends even if it means letting them go.

Where'd You Go, Bernadette, by Maria Semple (Alex 2013)

This family-centered adult novel is a teen favorite for its quirky humor, compelling narrative style, and the genuinely warm mother/daughter relationship it depicts. Eighth-grader Bee Branch requests a Christmas cruise to Antarctica as a reward for years of excellent grades, but after planning the trip in detail (thanks to a virtual assistant in India), her

---

Young adult books with particular appeal for adult readers are designated with a star (★).

mother, Bernadette, disappears right before their scheduled departure. Bernadette is devoted to Bee, but she is also a recluse who rarely leaves the house, and her Microsoft executive husband, Elgin, is planning to have her committed. It all comes together in a wacky yet moving denouement in which Elgin and Bee travel to Antarctica alone. The book moves quickly, because Bee's story is interspersed with a variety of other voices via e-mails, letters, report cards, documents, and an article about Bernadette's surprising past career.

Romance

Romance is a genre in which emotion is the primary appeal factor.[1] Teen love stories build from first impressions and the initial meeting, through shared experiences with the inevitable roadblocks, into resolution. Adult romance novels require a happy ending.[2] This is not necessarily true in teen romance, since teens are unlikely to find their life partner and are still learning about both relationships and themselves. Teens read the genre in order to experience romantic love (perhaps before they are ready for it themselves) and enjoy the adrenaline rush of attraction and the suspense of whether the other person feels it too, the excitement of reciprocation, and even the drama of conflict. Tone is crucial for romance readers, so it is important to pin down what a reader is seeking. Frothy? Tragic? Dreamy?

CORE TITLE

★*Eleanor & Park,* by Rainbow Rowell (Printz Honor, BFYA Top Ten, Odyssey Honor, AAYA Top Ten, TTT, QP 2014; Horn Book Award 2013)

In 1980s Omaha, overweight, redheaded new girl Eleanor and quiet, book-loving, half-Asian Park grudgingly sit next to each other on the bus to school. They begin sharing comics and mix-tapes during the ride and are both surprised as they gradually fall in love. Rowell creates a story that communicates just what hidden young love feels like: urgent, sweet, funny, yearning. Both Eleanor and Park feel incredibly fortunate and stunned to have found someone. But their relationship makes them targets, outsiders who are vulnerable to bullying. Eleanor also fears her abusive stepfather, while Park's stable home life becomes uncomfortable as he butts heads with his father. Short chapters, alternating first-person narrations, and great dialogue, along with the tension of Eleanor's precarious situation, make for compulsive reading. In their relationship the couple finds unconditional acceptance, sharp physical desire, and a measure of safety. But sometimes even the most sincere love is not enough to overcome the obstacles that life presents. Despite its 1980s setting, the appeal of this title places it firmly in the realistic romance genre.

NEXT READS

Anna and the French Kiss, by Stephanie Perkins (BFYA, PPYA 2012)

This dreamy escape read is set in Paris, where Anna is sent for a school year abroad. Most girls might swoon at this prospect, but Anna was looking forward to enjoying her senior year at home in Atlanta with her best friend Bridgette and pursuing a flirtation with her coworker. Besides, she's wary of her new city, since she speaks no French and has a fear of germs. But then she falls for Etienne St. Clair at first glance and is amazed to find that he shares her love of old movies. He seems interested in her, too, but he already has a girlfriend. Anna learns as much about herself and pursuing her dreams as she does about romance. The setting is a slam-dunk for appeal, and so are the fresh characters and smart dialogue.

Simon vs. the Homo Sapiens Agenda, by Becky Albertalli (Morris Award, BFYA Top Ten, AAYA 2016; NBA finalist 2015)

Simon, age sixteen, has been using a school computer to secretly exchange e-mails with a boy who calls himself Blue. Martin, a nerdy classmate, catches Simon at it, and blackmails him into persuading Abby, one of Simon's friends, to go out with Martin. This forces Simon to come to terms with his sexuality and to out himself to his friends and family. The reactions of his parents and teachers are complex and well developed, while Simon's insights into his own feelings are often funny, painful, and achingly real. And just who is this mysterious Blue? Simon guesses wrong a couple of times before Blue reveals himself and their romance is born. Readers cannot help but root for Simon as they, too, fall in love with his charm and humor. Movie version released in 2018.

The Sea of Tranquility, by Katja Millay (Alex 2014)

This adult novel of two older teens recovering from tragedy is an ideal crossover choice for teens. Nastya hasn't spoken in over a year. She was a piano prodigy until her hand was destroyed. Now Nastya lives in Florida with her aunt, where she hopes to start over and complete high school. Josh has lost his mother, father, and sister and is living alone in his family's house. Nastya, out for a run one night, is drawn to the garage where Josh is making a coffee table. Alternating first-person narratives reveal both characters in this emotional and suspenseful read. Will Nastya find her voice? Will she trust Josh enough to share what happened to her? As the two slowly grow closer, they learn that the intimacy of being loved requires healing and acceptance.

Pursuing Passions

Beyond schoolwork, friends, and family, most teens add several activities to their week, whether team sports, music, art, coding, the student council, the school newspaper, reading, writing, or theater. Pursuing a passion is one way to discover and develop a unique identity. It is also a way for teens to find people who share their interests: the people who become their tribe, support system, and friends. A special talent gives a teen confidence, but it can also mean expectations from parents, teachers, or coaches. Reading about others in these situations can be inspiring and reassuring.

CORE TITLE

I'll Give You the Sun, by Jandy Nelson (Printz Award, BFYA Top Ten 2015)

Before they lost their mother in a car accident, twins Jude and Noah were so close they were NoahandJude. In alternating chapters, Noah narrates the years before the accident and Jude the years after, when they are 13 and 16 respectively. Jude is a sculptor who attends the local arts academy, where Noah, a painter, is not accepted. This book is about art and creativity, but it is also about a betrayal that separates the twins, and how that rift begins to mend. Noah is deeply dramatic, and thrilled by his first gay crush. Jude is more cautious, and thinks often about her beloved grandmother and her superstitions. They are grieving, all the more painfully because they are doing so separately thanks to family secrets that are only slowly revealed. This is a long, carefully constructed literary novel, but its brilliant pace and deep emotionality never let the reader go, as passion cycles through its work and relationships. Readers who like smart books that make them feel deeply are the ideal audience here.

NEXT READS

The Disenchantments, by Nina LaCour (BFYA 2013)

Right after their high-school graduation, best friends Colby and Bev are headed out on tour with Bev's girl band, and then flying to Paris for a year of traveling the world together. But Bev chooses the first day of their road trip to share a secret with Colby—she's going to college after all, so she's not going to travel with him. Bev's revelation turns the trip more nostalgic than expected as Colby drives Bev and band members/sisters Meg and Alexa from San Francisco to Portland in his uncle's old VW van. Their tour lands them in some real dumps, but it also brings them closer together. For all the partying and freedom involved, this story focuses on relationships that will appeal to thoughtful readers, while also capturing the thrill of making music and expressing oneself, of being in the moment right before the next stage of life.

Dairy Queen, by Catherine Gilbert Murdock (BBYA 2007; PPYA 2014)

While most football books are dominated by male protagonists and authors, this one is quite the opposite. Ever since her older brothers left for college and her father broke his hip, D.J. has been doing the lion's share of work on the Wisconsin family farm. It's a huge daily burden, on top of which she takes on training the rival school's lazy but charming quarterback over the summer. D.J. loves football, and she's a genius at it. But in a family in which no one talks about anything, will she ever have a chance to pursue what she loves? Both the quirky plot and the humor of D.J.'s pitch-perfect, funny, self-deprecating voice make this book a true winner with tons of heart and soul.

Mexican WhiteBoy, by Matt de la Peña (BBYA 2009; PPYA 2013)

Questions of identity dog Daniel during his sixteenth summer, which he spends living with his Mexican cousin Sofia and her parents near the border. Daniel is half white and half Mexican, and is consequently an outsider both at his private school up north, and among his relatives. But he has amazing pitching skills. He didn't make the baseball team at school last year because he is too unreliable, but he excels at hustling players with his new friend Uno. They also bond over a common desire to reconnect with their absent fathers. Daniel falls in love with Liberty, a girl who only speaks Spanish, even though he never learned to speak it. The book's authentic street language feels raw but right, while Daniel's introspective thoughts and mental letters to his father communicate what he wishes the truth to be. Short chapters and good sports action keep the pace brisk enough for even the most reluctant readers.

Teens on the Edge

Today's teens struggle with everything from poverty and bullying to human trafficking, domestic violence, and drug abuse, and the boundary-pushing books being published for them reflect the daunting issues they face. Teens are attracted to these books because they crave the intensity of reading about terrifying situations or are curious about surviving them: they want to feel better about their own circumstances, they empathize with teens in terrible circumstances, or they are going through something themselves and need to feel less alone. Today's readers have access to a growing literature of sensitive, well-written titles addressing every issue imaginable by authors who bring hope and even levity to their stories through the authentic voices of their protagonists.

CORE TITLE

★*The Hate U Give*, by Angie Thomas (AAYA Top Ten, BFYA, QP Top Ten, Printz Honor 2018; Horn Book Award 2017)

In this novel inspired by the Black Lives Matter movement, sixteen-year-old Starr balances a loving home life with her family in Garden Heights, a mostly black urban neighborhood, and days spent at her suburban, mostly white prep school across town. One night she's being driven home from a party by a childhood friend, Khalil, when they are pulled over by a white police officer, and Khalil is shot to death. Starr is the only witness. Her world implodes, from clashes between protesters and police in her neighborhood, to testifying in front of a grand jury, to losing a close school friend who dismisses Khalil as an expendable drug dealer. Starr's first-person, present-tense narrative is pitch-perfect, the plot never slows, and Starr's extended family, friends, and white boyfriend are fully realized characters. Starr is empowered to speak up for justice, even though it endangers her safety and the safety of her family. This story provides a crucial window into several aspects of the contemporary black experience, and an equally important mirror for those living it.

NEXT READS

Dime, by E. R. Frank (BFYA 2016)

Dime lives in Newark, New Jersey, with a neglectful foster mother who has recently become abusive. Dime loves to read and is determined to stay in school. Then she meets L.A., who buys her warm food and talks with her. Eventually, L.A. takes her home, where she lives with Brandy and Daddy. Daddy makes Dime feel beautiful. He grooms her to join L.A. and Brandy as a prostitute, in exchange for living under his love and protection. Dime is completely taken in . . . until she isn't. She decides to rescue the other girls by writing the perfect letter to someone who will help. But whose voice should she use? She considers Sex (patterned after a novel she read once, narrated by Death). She considers Money, or Truth. Dime's words so immerse the reader in her situation that it seems inconceivable that this resourceful fourteen-year-old won't extricate herself from Daddy's grasp.

Some Girls Are, by Courtney Summers (BBYA, AAYA, QP Top Ten 2011; PPYA 2012)

Regina is on top of the world. She is Anna's best friend and she is dating Josh, who hosts all the best parties. One Friday night, Anna's boyfriend Donnie tries to rape Regina at a party. Regina tells their friend Kara, who advises her not to tell Anna what happened. On Monday morning, Regina realizes her mistake when she arrives at school to find that Kara has told Anna that Regina slept with Donnie behind her back. Kara is now Anna's best friend and Regina is a pariah. Physical, emotional, and online bullying push the limits of mean girl treatment. Despite unlikeable characters and uncomfortably intense situations, this is a popular novel thanks to well-executed short chapters, expert pacing, shocking violence, and Regina's realistic emotional journey. While Laurie Halse Anderson's *Speak* is for readers as young as eighth grade, this one appeals to older teens.

The Book of Unknown Americans, by Cristina Henriquez

In this book, the stories of two families living in an isolated apartment building in Delaware are brought to touching and dramatic life. Arturo and Alma Rivera left their happy and successful lives in Mexico to enroll their daughter, Maribel, in a special school in the United States after she suffered brain damage in an accident. Mayor, the son of their Panamanian neighbors, develops a deep interest in Maribel, in what devolves into a tragic Romeo and Juliet relationship.

The voices of several characters alternate through the book, bringing to life the frustrations and triumphs of starting over in a new country without knowing the language or understanding the details of everyday life. This is an intimate, heartbreaking story that will appeal to readers who enjoy emotional tearjerkers and want to understand and empathize with both the joy and tragedy of the immigrant experience in America.

Mental Illness

Teens are fascinated by characters living with mental illness, perhaps due to the combination of vulnerability and strength they exhibit, perhaps because some teens experience mood swings that make them wonder about their own mental health. Readers reach for these books in order to understand what a friend or family member is going through. It is important to suggest books in which mental illness is depicted in an accurate and realistic manner. And suicide, in particular, is an issue that demands careful handling in YA novels. Librarians need to be sure that the books they hand teens represent responsible portrayals.

CORE TITLE

All the Bright Places, by Jennifer Niven (BFYA, AAYA, TTT 2016; PPYA 2017)

Violet and Finch meet on the roof of their high school, where both are contemplating suicide. Finch is a legend for his extreme behavior. Every day he wakes up and decides whether today is the day to die. He fears losing time again—the five weeks of school before Christmas break were a long dark sleep. Violet was a cheerleader who dated the most popular boys before she lost her sister Eleanor in a car accident. Now she feels distant from her friends and suffers terrible nightmares. The book's chapters alternate between these two teens as they fall in love over a social studies project that has them visiting kitschy tourist sites in their home state of Indiana. For a while it seems like their relationship will be enough to save Finch, who is revealed to be bipolar. Several popular elements are done particularly well here. First, the reader cannot help but empathize with these characters. Their romance is not clichéd, and Finch's illness is unpredictable and heartbreaking, Violet's recovery is gradual and convincing, and the denouement is both affecting and satisfying.

NEXT READS

Challenger Deep, by Neal Shusterman (BFYA Top Ten, NBA Winner 2016; PPYA 2017; Horn Book Honor 2015)

Caden Bosch is a bright, creative teen who is descending into schizophrenia, unbeknownst to his friends and parents, who are increasingly baffled and alarmed by his behavior. Readers are taken inside Caden's mind via an unusual technique—every other chapter takes place on a pirate ship, where Caden interacts with the captain, his parrot, and others on board, and dreads their voyage into Challenger Deep. Readers feel increasingly lost in this intense story, just as Caden becomes more lost inside his thoughts, until he is placed in the hospital for treatment, the pirate ship is explained, and clarity gradually returns. The novel was inspired by the experiences of the author's son, Brendan, whose illustrations add an effective visual element to the story. Teens curious about how it feels to experience, and then cope with, a mental illness, will be captivated.

It's Kind of a Funny Story, by Ned Vizzini (BBYA 2007; PPYA 2017)

Craig is obsessed with getting into Manhattan's Executive Pre-Professional High School. When he passes the admissions test, he is sure his life will be perfect. But the academic pressure of attending is too much for him and he slips into depression. The reader gets quite a tour of Craig's mind. He has trouble eating and sleeping, and after going off his Zoloft prescription he decides to kill himself. Instead, he calls a Suicide Hotline and walks down the street to an emergency room, beginning five days spent in the psychiatric wing. These days are a whirlwind, filled with humor and heart, and teens will empathize with this boy who is so unsure of himself in so many areas of life. This is a welcome lighter, if emotional, portrayal of depression.

Wintergirls, by Laurie Halse Anderson (BBYA, TTT, QP 2010; PPYA 2016)

This bleak and at times disturbing novel gives readers an idea of how it feels to live with an eating disorder. Lia never answered the phone the night her ex-best friend, Cassie, called her thirty-three times. Then Cassie was found dead in a motel room. Cassie suffered from bulimia, and her friends even competed to see who could be the thinnest. Now, Cassie's death heightens Lia's own self-destructive behavior. Lia's lyrical, rich voice describes it all in this beautifully written, claustrophobic masterpiece in which logic sometimes gives way to stream-of-consciousness hallucinations. Fortunately, the ending is hopeful.

Even years after publication, this book remains the most striking and accurate portrayal of a teen suffering from an eating disorder, a category of mental illness that is about so much more than weight and body image.

Death and Dying

Books that address death and dying, and grief and loss are emotionally intense and often tearjerkers, even those that use humor to navigate these delicate waters, like *Life in a Fishbowl* by Len Vlahos. The key to their success is perhaps the fact that most books about death actually celebrate life and love. They encourage us to live in the moment, to face our mortality. John Green's *The Fault in Our Stars* was hardly the first book about a teen character with cancer, but its blockbuster popularity did kick off a continuing trend of terminal disease books for teen readers.

CORE TITLE

Everything, Everything, by Nicola Yoon (BFYA, QP Top Ten, TTT 2016)
> Madeline is ill with SCID (severe combined immunodeficiency); she can never leave the house for fear of the germs that lurk everywhere. She only has contact with her mother and her nurse, Carla. Madeline's father and brother were killed by a truck driver; she barely remembers them, but their loss has severely affected her mother. When Olly and his family move in next door, Madeline and Olly begin communicating, largely via text messages, until Carla allows them to meet—very carefully. Soon, Madeline is ready to break all the rules, to risk everything for the chance to experience just a little bit of what normal girls can have. The intensity of holding hands when one is never touched ... that is the root of the appeal here. That and a shocking plot twist that changes everything for Madeline. Madeline's sense of humor adds to the book's appeal, and short chapters make for a fast read, some comprising e-mails, texts, and illustrations. The 2017 film based on the novel is also hugely popular with teens.

NEXT READS

★*And We Stay,* by Jenny Hubbard (Printz Honor, BFYA 2015)
> Emily Beam is sent to a boarding school in the middle of her junior year after the suicide of her boyfriend, Paul. She is nearly overcome by guilt, wondering if her decision to break up with him following

an abortion caused Paul to shoot himself. Living in Amherst, where Emily Dickinson spent her life, our protagonist begins to write poetry in Dickinson's style, reflecting the past and her present recovery, even as the novel skips back in time to reveal the progression of her relationship with Paul, then returns to the present to depict boarding school life. Emily recovers hope thanks to a wonderful roommate, a supportive teacher, and her growing writing talent. This book's mixture of prose and pitch-perfect poetry appeals to teens who love to write themselves, and the author's sensitivity in portraying the events of the novel makes it bearable.

★*We Are Okay*, by Nina LaCour (Printz Award, BFYA 2018)

Marin is reeling from the death of her Gramps back in California when she arrives at college in upstate New York. Marin is an orphan, having lost her mother to a surfing accident when she was only three, and she never knew her father. The novel begins as the dorm empties out for the winter break, and Marin waits for the arrival of her best friend, Mabel. Marin hasn't answered any of Mabel's texts or calls since she left California in the fall, and she doesn't know how to handle her visit, since they had shared the summer as more than friends. This book is also about a surprising betrayal that leaves Marin feeling utterly alone. Sensitive readers who enjoy literary writing and deep character portrayals are the perfect audience for this intimate novel with its tearjerker of a cathartic ending.

Alice Bliss, by Laura Harrington

In this outstanding adult crossover novel, Alice Bliss, age fourteen, lives in an idyllic small American town with her parents and her younger sister, Ellie. Her father loves his work, coaches Little League, and joins the Army Reserve. When his unit is called up for active duty and he is deployed to Iraq, Alice's mother cannot function. She stops shopping, cooking, and cleaning. Alice takes to wearing her father's blue shirt every day for weeks, but she also manages to get Ellie fed and into bed each night, as well as walked to school each morning, with the help of the boy next door and her best friend, Henry. Alice also turns to Henry for comfort after her father is declared missing in action. The loss of a parent is surely one of the most difficult things a child can endure. Here it is presented without cloying sentiment, terrible but survivable.

Expanding Readers' Horizons
into the Whole Collection

Movies

Clueless

This romp retells Jane Austen's *Emma* in 1990s Beverly Hills.

The Fault in Our Stars

This heartbreaker about two teen cancer patients who fall in love is a faithful adaptation of the blockbuster novel by John Green.

If I Stay

Mia, a cellist on her way to Juilliard, suffers injuries that put her in a coma. This film is based on the novel by Gayle Forman.

A Monster Calls

A young teen finds himself talking with a tree monster after his single mother is diagnosed with terminal cancer. Patrick Ness wrote the screenplay himself.

The Perks of Being a Wallflower

Based on the beloved novel by Stephen Chbosky, freshman introvert Charlie is befriended by two seniors, who help him get through the suicide of his best friend and his own mental illness.

Television

Many of the shows listed here have finished airing, since realistic television is not the current trend.

The Fosters

Siblings Callie and Jude are placed in foster care with a lesbian couple.

Friday Night Lights

This show follows the football coach, players, and cheerleaders in the small town of Dillon, Texas.

Gilmore Girls

This is centered on the relationship between a single mother and her teenage daughter. Its popularity flared again with the more recent *Gilmore Girls: A Year in the Life*.

Glee

>The high school glee club becomes a home for a variety of misfits. This show features covers of popular songs.

Gossip Girls

>Upper East Side Manhattan teens are dogged by a stalker blogger who is reporting their every move.

Grey's Anatomy

>Teens cannot get enough of this medical drama.

One Tree Hill

>High school kids in a small North Carolina town are obsessed with its basketball team.

Thirteen Reasons Why

>Based on the novel by Jay Asher, this was a huge hit, but it also fostered serious concerns about its treatment of teen suicide.

Recommendations for Readers' Advisory

For those new to young adult literature, it will be very helpful to obtain a grounding in the most popular authors (Rainbow Rowell, John Green, Sarah Dessen, and Nicola Yoon for starters), and to keep a list of read-alikes for their books. To keep these lists updated, it is important to add to them in the process of reading reviews and working with teens. It is also helpful to keep an eye on authors who have a loud fan following, and seem poised to break into this category (perhaps Becky Albertalli, Adam Silvera, or Jason Reynolds).

Adult librarians just getting their feet wet may be surprised at how intense and complex realistic fiction for teens can be, especially titles that address social issues or illness. This genre is full of appeal for adult readers, and adult readers who are new to the books written for this age group may enjoy reading popular titles more than they expected. A great strategy is to scaffold read-alikes and appeal thoughts using crossover authors that adults know well, such as Jodi Picoult, Kristin Hannah, Maria Semple, and Emma Straub.

If the same teen patrons ask over and over again for suggestions for realistic fiction, it makes sense to expand into memoirs and autobiographies. They have a similar appeal and can be very popular with teens. See the "Nonfiction" chapter for more details.

"Windows and mirrors," as lightly referenced in the Appeal section of this chapter, has become a standard concept in multicultural literature for readers' advisors working with children and teens. All children need to see themselves reflected in the books they read, in order to feel seen and valued (i.e., mirrors). Children also need to see characters who reflect people very different from themselves in the books they read, in order to expand their worldview (i.e., windows). This terminology was coined by Rudine Sims Bishop in her 1990 essay "Mirrors, Windows and Sliding Glass Doors,"[3] and it became even more widely known when a 2016 TED Talk by Grace Lin based on the concept was shared widely on social media.[4]

A book will be a window or mirror depending on an individual reader's personal background and experiences. It is not necessary for the readers' advisor to determine *why* a reader is seeking a particular book, if it is indeed a window or a mirror for them. But it is important that multicultural portrayals are accurate, positive, and respectful. Therefore, librarians need to know about the best books to hand to patrons, and to do so tactfully and respectfully.

Keeping Up with New and Upcoming Titles

Because the majority of diverse titles are realistic, I am highlighting diversity resources here. For even more, see the listings in chapter 4.

Journals

Best Books of the Year lists from *Booklist, School Library Journal, Kirkus Reviews, Publishers Weekly*, and *Horn Book*.

Websites

Disability in Kidlit: http://disabilityinkidlit.com/

Diversity in YA: http://diversityinya.tumblr.com/

Teen Librarian Toolbox: www.teenlibrariantoolbox.com/

This blog, sponsored by *School Library Journal*, is full of book reviews and lists, which are particularly strong in realistic fiction.

We Need Diverse Books: https://diversebooks.org/

Awards and Lists

Amelia Bloomer Book List: https://ameliabloomer.wordpress.com/
 Notable feminist literature for birth to age eighteen, administered by the Feminist Task Force of the Social Responsibilities Round Table of the American Library Association. The fiction list is predominantly realistic.

In the Margins Book Award & Selection Committee:
www.youthlibraries.org/margins-book-award-selection-committee
 Mostly edgy selections belonging in the "Teens on the Edge" subgenre, chosen by Library Services for Youth in Custody (LSYC).

Rainbow Book List: GLBTQ Books for Children and Teens:
http://glbtrt.ala.org/rainbowbooks/rainbow-books-lists
 Books with significant and authentic GLBTQ content, administered by the Gay, Lesbian, Bisexual, and Transgender Round Table of the American Library Association.

Rita Award: https://www.rwa.org/p/cm/ld/fid=535
 Romance Writers of America awards include a Young Adult Romance category.

We're the People: https://wtpsite.wordpress.com/
 An annual summer reading list of books written or illustrated by Native Americans or people of color, including characters who are people of color or Native, people with disabilities, or LGBTQ people.

Where to Find Diverse Books (from the We Need Diverse Books website): https://diversebooks.org/resources/where-to-find-diverse-books/
 A place to find even more book awards and lists.

Print Resources

Cart, Michael, and Christine A. Jenkins. *Top 250 LGBTQ Books for Teens: Coming Out, Being Out, and the Search for Community.* Chicago: Huron Street, 2016.

Jensen, Karen. "Tackling Mental Health through YA Lit." *School Library Journal.* November 2015. www.slj.com/2015/11/teens-ya/tackling-mental-health-through-ya-lit/#_.

Jensen, Kelly. *It Happens: A Guide to Contemporary Realistic Fiction for the YA Reader*. Bowie, MD: VOYA, 2014.

Moulton, Erin. "Books That Help." *School Library Journal*. November 2014. www.slj.com/2014/11/teens-ya/bibliotherapy-for-teens -helpful-tips-and-recommended-fiction/#_.

Wadham, Rachel. *This Is My Life: A Guide to Realistic Fiction for Teens*. Santa Barbara, CA: Libraries Unlimited, 2010.

NOTES

1. Joyce G. Saricks, *The Readers' Advisory Guide to Genre Fiction*, 2nd ed. (Chicago: American Library Association, 2009), 131.
2. Ibid, 132.
3. This essay was originally published in *Perspectives* 1, no. 3: ix–xi. Sims speaks about the concept here: https://www.youtube.com/watch?v=_AAu58SNSyc.
4. Grace Li, "The Windows and Mirrors of Your Child's Bookshelf," YouTube, posted by TEDxNatick, March 18, 2016, https://www.youtube.com/ watch?v=_wQ8wiV3FVo.

7

Science Fiction

cience fiction is a speculative literature of "What if?" and it answers that question based on science rather than pure imagination. One useful definition comes from the sci-fi grand master Arthur C. Clarke: "Science fiction is something that *could* happen—but you usually wouldn't want it to. Fantasy is something that *couldn't* happen—though you often only wish that it could."[1] Joyce Saricks expands on this: "Science Fiction posits worlds and technologies which could exist. Science, rather than magic, drives these speculative tales, and the science must be accurate and true to key axioms of Newtonian (classical) and relativistic physics."[2]

Reading science fiction is a complete escape from daily life, but it is not a mindless one. Attention must be paid to the parameters of the story from the very first paragraphs, as the reader acclimates to a book's world. While horror, for example, transports its readers with emotion (dread or fear), science fiction will more likely spark curiosity and wonder, even consternation, as the reader figures out just where and when the book is set. Some science fiction books have gentle beginnings that allow the reader to get to know a character or begin to gather clues about the setting. Others drop the reader into the middle of an action set-piece and use the energy of the writing (and even, perhaps, a strange new vocabulary) to carry readers through the first chapter.

Because of the hurdles of acclimating to new worlds and new ideas in each book, many teens assume that they are not interested in science fiction. They may not realize that they have been fans of science fiction all along, thanks to beloved classics like *A Wrinkle in Time* and *The Giver,* or Rebecca Stead's *When You Reach Me.* This is the genre that encompasses dystopian novels, which were the most widely loved stories in teen literature for several years, and are still popular. The ubiquity of *Hunger Games* read-alikes, for example, encouraged many to overcome their prejudice against the genre, especially since romance inserted itself into the story.

Science fiction is the genre of huge franchises like *Star Trek* and *Star Wars* that have influenced generations of fans and creators alike. Summer movie blockbusters are often members of the genre—all the way back to *E.T., Close Encounters of the Third Kind*, and *2001: A Space Odyssey.* Science fiction tropes are so well known that *Guardians of the Galaxy* was able to poke fun at and celebrate them. These movies draw in even the most skeptical teens with humor, friendship, and a childlike sense of wonder.

Science fiction is the genre of *The Hunger Games, The Maze Runner,* and *Divergent*; these book and movie blockbuster series have spawned huge fandoms. Teens who self-identify as participants in geek culture love shows like *Doctor Who.* Teens participate in cosplay (costume play) events, attend Comic-Cons, and play video games inspired by science fiction for hours. Science fiction fandom can give outsider teens a fun, unique geek identity.

Appeal

In her essay "All about Science Fiction for Teens," Jennifer Stubben Hatch states that "the best science fiction offers thoughtful and provocative examinations of how our present society may evolve, both culturally and technologically."[3] Science fiction gives teens a fresh way to view the world they live in and the issues that concern them, like inequality and environmental problems. Perceptive teens who think deeply about our world are some of science fiction's biggest fans.

On the opposite end of the spectrum are readers who come to science fiction for a book that allows their imaginations to soar beyond the everyday. Traditionally, the appeal of science fiction is said to be largely intellectual. However, many popular young-adult science fiction titles are adrenaline-filled, and share the escapist appeal of thrillers or fast-paced survival tales. Therefore, our examination of the genre is not limited to the traditional definition of science fiction. We will take each subgenre and book on its own terms.

Setting

World-building is arguably the most prominent appeal element in science fiction. What is unusual about this world? Has the world run out of water? Has virtual reality become a refuge? Authors may use strange language and new vocabulary as an element of world-building, which might deter novice readers. But the best novelists don't give their readers a chance to escape. One example is M. T. Anderson's *Feed,* in which the slang used by teens traveling to the Moon for spring break sets up character, tone, and setting simultaneously.

Pacing

Pacing can be used to keep readers moving through any initial strangeness they encounter. Adapting is easier when the reader is immersed in a chase scene or a grand heist. In Philip Reeve's *Mortal Engines,* the hero runs (literally) to reach his home, the great traction city of London. Some of the most popular books throw readers into the middle of a set-piece and let them find out about the world as the story hurtles forward.

Tone

Tone is crucial. Is a teen looking for something madcap? Bleak? Heroic? Warm? Funny? Many science fiction novels are bleak, pitting a young underdog against a heartless corporation or a destructive alien society. Maybe that's why humor is so popular in science fiction. Books like *The Hitchhiker's Guide to the Galaxy* and John Scalzi's *Redshirts* send up common tropes, while Andy Weir's *The Martian* uses humor to lighten a hopeless situation. Joss Whedon's *Firefly* was (and is) a huge hit because of its sense of humor, as well as the love and loyalty within its (often bickering) crew.

Character

Science fiction is perhaps less interested in character development than other genres, but there are inspired exceptions. Consider Katniss in *The Hunger Games,* and the strong characters who followed her. Many YA science fiction novels feature a heroic teen who goes above and beyond what others (especially adults) are willing to do, or is particularly perceptive and thinks for himself.

Story/Theme

Science fiction is often about ideas or problems, particularly ethical dilemmas. *I, Robot* considers the wisdom of developing artificial intelligence. *The Adoration of Jenna Fox* questions the wisdom of bioengineering. Dystopian fiction raises moral questions about race, age, poverty, medical ethics, and more. Placing today's issues in a different setting highlights society's challenges in ways that excite teens about changing the world for the better.

Key Subgenres and Core Titles in Science Fiction

Space Opera

Adventurous space exploration or colonization sagas (like *Star Trek* and *Star Wars*) often include plenty of humor, fresh ideas, and a heavy dose of camaraderie. Part of their appeal is a peek into alien cultures and planets. Science fiction is self-referential, so reading the classics of sci-fi is crucial for avid fans. For example, *Dune* is at the center of a lot of conversation, and still appears on top-selling science fiction lists.[4] Many of these titles have dystopian or post-apocalyptic elements, since the need to explore beyond Earth often reflects a need to find a safer or more livable world.

CORE TITLE

Illuminae, by Amie Kaufman and Jay Kristoff (BFYA, AAYA, TTT 2016)

A mining colony is attacked by a commercial rival in this unusual space adventure. Kady (a welcome female protagonist in a largely male-dominated subgenre) escapes Kerenza IV on one of three ships that make it out; her mother and her ex-boyfriend Ezra make it onto another. Then their attacker sends a dreadnought to destroy the survivors. The chase narrative turns darker as the artificial intelligence that controls one ship malfunctions, a deadly virus spreads on another, and Kady (a computer prodigy) discovers shocking secrets of betrayal while hacking into ship systems. On the page this book's narrative is visually intriguing, made up of e-mail, instant messages, interview transcripts, and discovered security footage, as well as graphic representations of space battles and artificial intelligence malfunctions. Even readers who dislike romance will be moved by Kady and Ezra's progression from bitter exes to fellow warriors to something deeper, all while on separate ships and fighting for survival. An unexpected plot twist sends this thrill ride in unexpected, emotionally devastating directions. The multi-narrator (twenty of them!) audiobook is particularly excellent. This is the first title in the *Illuminae Files* series.

NEXT READS

Black Hole Sun, by David Macinnis Gill

Durango is the sixteen-year-old leader of a group of outcast Regulators (i.e., mercenaries) who are getting paid to save miners on Mars from a terrifying enemy—cannibals called the Draeu. Durango has a secret (about his father), and a huge chip on his shoulder as a result. His former leader from Battle School, Mimi, was mortally wounded in battle and is now integrated into his brain. Durango consults her constantly; their sarcastic banter is a highlight of the book. It all comes down to medical experiments gone tragically wrong. This book is particularly accessible to genre newbies thanks to humorous dialogue, over-the-top action scenes, short chapters, thriller pacing, and familiar echoes of *Star Wars*—and even the James Bond films. The language is sprinkled with new words that are easy to figure out in context, many of them funny or slightly blasphemous. This is the first book in a trilogy.

A Confusion of Princes, by Garth Nix (BFYA 2013)

Although this novel is told in the first person and is largely plot-driven, Nix trusts his readers to handle some complicated world-building. Prince Khemri comes of age believing he is destined to become Emperor, but he is actually one of ten million princes, and is vulnerable to assassination attempts. It might take a more experienced teen science-fiction reader to acclimate to this world and Khemri's many encounters and travels. Great enhancement technology, both biological and psychological, as well as space travel and battles, will keep these readers very happy. Love for the author's popular *Abhorsen* series may lead fantasy fans to this book as well. There is some diversity here, thanks to Khemri's brown skin, and this is a rare stand-alone book in a genre full of series.

Lockstep, by Karl Schroeder

This adult novel is an accessible stand-alone space opera starring seventeen-year-old Toby, whose ship is breached, placing him in hibernation. He wakes up 14,000 years later to find that his family rules the Lockstep, a group of worlds that hibernates 360 months for every one month awake, and that he has become an integral part of Lockstep's religion as it developed. Readers have several fascinating lockstep worlds to experience via Toby's adventures as he tries to connect with (and then survive) his family. This is very much a plot- and concept-driven book, in which character and emotion take a back seat. *Lockstep* is a book for teens who are ready to wrap their minds around the effects on society of the enforced hibernation cycle (especially on those who refuse and rebel).

Virtual Reality

Science fiction based in virtual worlds is largely fast-paced and action-based. Think of quests undertaken by geeky, unpopular boys who show their bravery in these alternate universes. A large part of the subgenre's appeal is one of creative puzzle-solving, and traveling through imaginative, unexpected landscapes and situations. These novels can feel like playing a game, and they often incorporate game-playing itself. But most of these books bring play into a more serious, survival-dependent realm before long, in order to raise the stakes. Unlike the real world, where the movements of teens are limited, in virtual worlds their lives are flexible.

CORE TITLE

Ready Player One, by Ernest Cline (Alex 2012)

Wade Watts, an obsessive gamer, lives in a near-future America where people spend most of their time in OASIS, a globally networked virtual world. When James Halliday, the Willy Wonka-like creator of OASIS, dies, a video message announces that the first person to find the "Easter egg" hidden inside OASIS will inherit his fortune. Finding it involves solving three riddles and playing (and winning) numerous games, many of them video and arcade games from the 1980s. It is five years before anyone makes progress, and that person is Wade. Other top contenders include his best friend, Aech, and a mysterious girl, Art3mis. The pace moves fast, taking the reader from one cultural icon to another—Saturday morning cartoons, movies, books, video games (of course), and music. The novel takes readers on a quest with a huge reward, and solving the riddles turns into a life-or-death struggle against wealthy, deceitful corporations. The appeal of this novel goes far beyond teen geeks, and fortunately, the 1980s references do not prevent today's readers from enjoying the humor and adventure.

NEXT READS

Warcross, by Marie Lu (BFYA, QP 2018)

Bounty hunter Emika Chen is barely making ends meet in a future New York City. Orphaned at twelve years old, she spent time in foster care and has a juvenile record. Now nineteen, Emika is desperately behind on paying the rent and days away from homelessness. She sees her chance during the opening ceremony of the biggest event of the year—a worldwide championship tournament that takes place inside a popular virtual reality called Warcross. Chen uses a programming breach to sneak into the tournament and steal a power-up worth thousands of dollars. Her plan goes awry, but instead of being arrested she is flown by private jet to Tokyo by Warcross creator Hideo Tanaka. Tanaka offers Emika a job to apprehend a hacker threatening Warcross from within. Seamless worldbuilding eases readers into a thrilling plot full of intrigue, hackers, video games, and even romance. Emika is an engaging protagonist, sympathetic yet tough.

Bubble World, by Carol Snow

This is a sparkling comic take on living in a virtual reality. Freesia spends her days on the island of Agalinas, going to high school to accumulate points, which she spends on beautiful clothes. All teens in Agalinas use fun vocabulary like *de-vicious* and *squiggy*, are surrounded by product placements, and attend a different themed party every night. Unfortunately, a tech glitch sends Freesia (nee Francine) back home to Phoenix, Arizona, and her real family. She is appalled by her plain face and lumpy body after three years inhabiting her gorgeous avatar. When she realizes that the corporation is feeding her friends memory blockers instead of education and she fights back, she is stranded permanently in the real world, where she learns to live an authentic life.

Lock In, by John Scalzi (Alex Award 2015)

This adult novel blend of science fiction, mystery, and corporate thriller introduces a near future transformed by the spread of Haden's Syndrome. This virus has killed millions and left others locked in their minds, unable to move or control their bodies. These victims can interact with the world via a virtual environment, and in the real world via robots called threeps. There are also recovered Haden victims who are Integrators, who can allow their bodies to be controlled by others. Chris Shane, a rookie FBI agent and Haden survivor, and his veteran partner Leslie Vann are assigned a murder investigation that has political and technological implications for Integrators. Chris and Leslie have great chemistry, the action is fast-paced, and the disability politics will interest socially conscious readers.

Military Science Fiction

The appeals of this subgenre are many. There is the big picture of thinly veiled commentary on current events and politics, the adrenaline of battles in space (where teens vicariously enjoy the glory of victory), and the methodical calculation of political strategizing. Not to mention cool far-future technologies and alien foes. For other readers, it is the more personal effect of war on the soldiers and their loved ones. Some consider Robert Heinlein's novel *Starship Troopers* to be the first example of military science fiction, and it remains a good suggestion for teens.

CORE TITLE

Ender's Game, by Orson Scott Card (Hugo, Nebula; PPYA 2015)

Andrew "Ender" Wiggin is sent to Battle School to learn tactics for defeating the hostile alien "buggers" that are determined to destroy the Earth. Ender faces intense pressure to perform from his superiors, and equally intense bullying and jealousy from his peers once his military genius begins to manifest itself. A twist lends Ender's story an emotional depth that resonates with teens. There is action, dysfunctional family dynamics, and an ending that turns Ender's triumph into a deep well of sadness and guilt, which lends this book even greater appeal to teens who are reading for more than just the thrills of the virtual battle scenes. The 2012 movie adaptation does not do the book justice, but there is a good graphic novel version illustrated by Pasqual Ferry (Marvel, 2013). *Ender's Game* is a great entry into science fiction for teens, and only the first in a series. Also within the Ender universe is the *Shadow* series, which follows Ender's Battle School classmate, Bean, another underdog. Young readers especially enjoy this series.

NEXT READS

Insignia, by S. J. Kincaid (BFYA 2013)

Tom goes from being a slacker virtual reality gamer who skips school to a potential war hero after he is recruited by General Marsh to join a training program for teens. World War III is being fought in space, using unmanned craft controlled from a distance. Teens are the combatants of choice because their brains adapt to the neural implant that every trainee must accept. And Tom loves it. The implant transforms his thinking, feeding everything directly into his brain—the morning wakeup alarm, school lessons, even the name and rank of everyone he meets. (What could possibly go wrong?) Trainees learn battle strategy in virtual simulations that are the highlight of the book. *Insignia* is not about character-building, and even the world-building is fairly nebulous. Its ideas about brain science, warfare, corporate control, and government betrayal make it work. This is the first book in the *Insignia* trilogy.

★*The Knife of Never Letting Go,* by Patrick Ness (BFYA 2009; AAYA Top Ten, Odyssey Honor, PPYA 2011; James Tiptree, Jr. Award)

Todd and his dog, Manchee, encounter a silence in the swamp just outside town, which should be impossible thanks to the Noise, the inescapable cacophony of everyone's thoughts. Todd is the youngest person in Prentisstown (population 147). All the women died when the native population, the Spackle, "released the Noise germ during the war." Todd is able to hide the silence from Mayor Prentiss for a short time. But soon after Todd figures out that the silence is a girl, Viola, who survived the crash landing of a colonizing ship they are discovered. Todd and Viola flee, barely one step ahead of the Mayor. This book's world-building is excellent, the suspense is high, the plot revelations are perfectly paced, and comic relief is provided by Manchee. As it progresses, the *Chaos Walking* trilogy becomes a harsh, bleak commentary on war.

Robopocalypse, by Daniel H. Wilson (Alex 2012)

Perhaps the scientists in *I, Robot* who feared the development of artificial intelligence (AI) had it right, for this adult novel examines one way those fears might play out. In the near future, a computer scientist developing AI decides to "kill" his latest program. The computer, Athos, has other ideas, and the Robot Wars begin. Briefing reports found after the war detail the heroic actions of the characters who first deprogram the computers and then find and attack Athos's arctic lair. The story emphasizes battle rather than the science and philosophy of AI, so we recommend this book to readers who enjoy full-throttle action. Wilson wrote two related humorous books that are perfect for teens, *How to Survive a Robot Uprising* (Bloomsbury, 2005) and *How to Build a Robot Army* (Bloomsbury, 2007).

Young adult books with particular appeal for adult readers are designated with a star (★).

Steampunk

Steampunk fiction is a subgenre whose historical settings feature steam-powered machinery from the nineteenth century instead of advanced technology. The highlight of steampunk science fiction is world-building, not only the setting but the reinvented technologies and Victorian-inspired fashions that populate it. Most of these novels walk a fine line between science fiction and fantasy, but when the machines (dirigibles, automatons, time machines) are largely the point, then I'm recommending them here. For teens who want to get acclimated to the subgenre, hand them *Steampunk! An Anthology of Fantastically Rich and Strange Stories,* edited by Gavin J. Grant and Kelly Link.

CORE TITLE

★*Mortal Engines,* by Philip Reeve (BBYA 2004)

In this future Europe, towns and cities move on wheels—called "traction cities"—and London is the greatest of them all. It is the era of Municipal Darwinism—cities devour each other, the winner ingesting (i.e., putting to use) every bit of the loser as it is dismantled. Tom is an orphan apprentice working at the London Museum. Hester is a disfigured girl whose family was killed by Valentine, London's head historian. When Hester tries to exact her revenge, she succeeds in getting them both kicked out of the city and onto the surface. Their race to get back into London takes them on amazing, frightening adventures. This book is the perfect combination of ideas and action. Reeve is a master at doling out mysteries at a good pace, keeping his characters moving and keeping the suspense tight, all within a fascinating, unique world. This book is the first in the *Hungry City Chronicles Series*; fans will also want to track down the prequel trilogy (in which the idea for traction cities is born and slowly becomes a reality), beginning with *Fever Crumb.*

NEXT READS

★*Airborn,* by Kenneth Oppel (Printz Honor, BBYA, QP 2005; PPYA 2011)

Matt works as a cabin boy on board the *Aurora,* a luxury airship—imagine a dirigible crossed with a multistory cruise ship. Matt is high in the crow's nest when he spies a failing hot air balloon and takes part in a daring rescue. The balloon captain's dying words are about mysterious flying, furry beasts, which must be hallucinations.

The main story takes place one year later when the balloon captain's granddaughter comes aboard seeking the truth. This story is elegantly told, and Matt is a solid, hard-working young man who wants nothing more than to follow in his father's footsteps and climb the ranks on the *Aurora*. *Airborn* takes place during an alternate Victorian era, and incorporates pirates and comic relief, which make it a much lighter read than *Mortal Engines,* and a good choice for younger teens. This is the first book in the *Airborn* trilogy.

Incarceron, by Catherine Fisher (BBYA, AAYA 2011; PPYA 2012)

Incarceron was a prison built to be a utopia, which instead became sentient and morphed over time into a living hell for the prisoners who are born, live, and die there. Now, centuries later, Incarceron watches over its inhabitants; no one ever leaves and no one can get in. Those born on the Outside live in a world where humans exist as if in medieval times, eschewing technology and advancements of any kind. Only the warden knows the truth about the prison. His daughter, Claudia, steals one of the two crystal keys that connect the inside and outside worlds. A young inmate, Finn, finds the other key. This book is both an adventure story and a philosophical look at imprisonment and society, and it is different from anything else out there. It is the first book in a duology.

Leviathan, by Scott Westerfeld (BBYA, AAYA 2010; Locus YA)

In an alternate World War I, there are two camps, the Darwinists and Clankers. The Darwinists genetically manipulate living, breathing organisms into war machines. The Clankers use mechanical technology to build them. Two fifteen-year-olds on opposite sides of the war meet: one is a cross-dressing girl serving inside a flying whaleship named Leviathan, while the other is a prince on the run maneuvering a Stormwalker, a machine that walks on two legs. Adrenaline and suspense rule the appeal here, through constant battle scenes between the two sides. But world-building, and the appeal of alternate history, are well-served, too. The world-building is heightened by intricate black-and-white illustrations that help readers visualize the author's unique creations.

Time Travel

The novels featured here are firmly based in our world, and use science—not fantasy—as the basis of time travel. Time travel that looks forward offers a peek at the future. The appeal of time travel that looks backward often lies in the power of second chances. It uses familiar history to engage readers even while blowing their minds with the differences that can result from the tiniest alteration in the past. Time travel's readership may intersect with historical fiction. This subgenre tends to include large doses of romance.

CORE TITLE

★*All Our Yesterdays,* by Cristin Terrill (BFYA 2014)

Em and Finn return to the present day from the future determined to stop the creation of a time machine named Cassandra. They have failed fourteen times. Only one strategy remains—killing their friend James. In the present, Miranda, James, and Finn are friends, and are all dressed up to attend a political fund-raising dinner where James's older brother and guardian, Nate, is scheduled to speak. But Nate is assassinated on stage. Who shot him, and why? What is so terrible about the future, and how will destroying Cassandra prevent it? Are they justified in killing one man in order to save a civilization? Other heavy themes, including global politics and the roots of evil, are balanced by a strong romance. Convincing character development is also central, and just how an innocent teen might become an evil adult. A tight, intriguing plot and confident writing create an engrossing reading experience for teens who are up for philosophy wrapped in a thriller.

NEXT READS

The Here and Now, by Ann Brashares

Prenna and her mom are immigrants from the 2090s, a time of plague and climate extremes. They come to present-day New York with the goal of changing the decline of the Earth's environment. They are required to join our culture without anyone guessing that they are from another time, and they are not allowed to become close to anyone. Prenna breaks that rule by starting a romance with her classmate Ethan. This relationship becomes the primary focus of the book, though the plot also includes a murder and a mystery. Time travel and romance most definitely do mix, and teens love Brashares's books. This is a good gateway for teens who are not usually tempted by time travel fare.

The Time Traveler's Wife, by Audrey Niffenegger (Alex 2004)

This hugely popular adult novel follows one couple, their separate lives, and their great love for each other. Clare and Henry meet over and over again, but every time Henry is a different age, and has dropped in from a random time and place. He has Chrono-Displacement Disorder and cannot control when and where he will time travel. Clare's life progresses normally, so they are rarely in the same place at the same age. This deeply romantic story is not without its tragedies, and the angst of the situation is part of its appeal. The modern-day Chicago setting is especially effective, so teens in that region may particularly appreciate the novel.

Kindred, by Octavia Butler

Dana, a black woman at home in 1976 Los Angeles, suddenly finds herself on a riverbank saving the life of a young boy. Over the following hours, she realizes that she is in nineteenth-century Maryland, during slavery times, and is being treated as such. She returns to modern Los Angeles when her life is threatened, but only hours later she finds herself back in the past, and this time the boy she saved, Rufus, is a little older, and is about to fall out of a tree. And the time after this, he's older still, setting fire to his room. Dana uncovers that Rufus is one of her ancestors, and she has to keep him alive long enough to have a child, or Dana will never be born. Witnessing a modern woman live as a slave is shocking, and provides insights into both the past and our present. Teens interested in race will be riveted, because even though this adult classic is slow in pace, it is great in suspense.

Humor

Finding the perfect funny book for a patron is a constant challenge. Science fiction holds several treasures. In the case of spoofs and parodies, readers need to have some SF experience to appreciate an author's humor. But sometimes it's all in the read. It's worth noting that there are more examples of humor lurking within other parts of this chapter. Check out *Black Hole Sun* for its witty banter, *Grasshopper Jungle* for sheer bravado, and *Bubble World* for its cleverly vapid vocabulary. The titles listed here are all adult books that were quickly appropriated by young adult readers.

CORE TITLE

The Martian, by Andy Weir (Alex 2015)

A small team of astronauts on the third manned NASA mission to Mars is overtaken by a violent dust storm. As the crew struggles to return to their landing vehicle, Mark Watley is struck by a flying antenna that pierces his suit and knocks out him far from the others. Luckily for Watley, he survives. But there are a few problems: he's been left behind on Mars, everyone thinks he's dead, and he has no way to communicate with them. Watley, a mechanical engineer and botanist, immediately begins working out how to stay alive. His problem-solving skills and ability to "fix broken stuff" are astounding, but he needs to be rescued before his life-support systems wear down or his food runs out. The story is told mostly through Watley's hilarious end-of-day log entries, which are full of humor and humanity, frustration and determination. At the same time, the reader is kept on the edge of her seat while NASA and Watley's former crew figure out how to save him in time. The 2015 award-winning movie version of this book is also very popular with teens.

NEXT READS

The Hitchhiker's Guide to the Galaxy, by Douglas Adams

This cult classic is a huge favorite among certain teen readers, regardless of their usual genres of preference. (Just like with adults, the book's humor either hits just right or not at all.) Arthur Dent is the only survivor of Earth and is now on a journey around the galaxy, a journey full of absurd encounters with aliens both friendly and otherwise. The utter silliness of the book's humor combines with satirical insight and riffs on humanity's role in the universe. This is a possible recommendation for teens who enjoy *Doctor Who*, and vice versa. Watchers of *Monty Python* and readers of Terry Pratchett's *Discworld* novels may enjoy this as well. There are many British expressions that will be lost on American teens, but those who love the book will not care. This is the first book in a series.

The Eyre Affair, by Jasper Fforde (Alex 2003)

This quirky, British alternate history is full of wordplay, time travel, crime, and even a little romance. Thursday Next is a wonderful protagonist who is brave, self-deprecating, and smart. She is a literary detective for Special Ops, and her current assignment is to capture Acheron Hades, a terribly charming villain who has gone from killing police officers to killing off literary characters. I'm always amazed by how much teens love this book, even those who haven't read the novels that it centers on, including *Jane Eyre*. Those who have read it swoon to meet Mr. Rochester in person. Characters like Thursday's uncle Mycroft and her father, who is constantly appearing out of nowhere to check on the status of the Crimean War, add a wonderful wackiness to the proceedings. This book is the first in a series.

William Shakespeare's Star Wars: Verily, a New Hope, by Ian Doescher (AAYA Top Ten 2014)

Spoofs and parodies on well-known science-fiction classics are great fun. Doescher retells the *Star Wars* movie in five acts using Shakespearean language and stage directions, accompanied by black-and-white illustrations. Young Shakespeare fans might even recognize parallels to famous speeches from the perennially assigned plays *Hamlet, Macbeth,* and *Romeo and Juliet.* But the appeal here is mostly for the quick laugh. Readers enjoy browsing this book for the best lines. What could be better than the words of Darth Vader (or the bleeps of R2-D2) in iambic pentameter? The full-cast audiobook is a YALSA Amazing Audiobooks Top Ten. The *William Shakespeare's Star Wars* series is six volumes in all, one for each original *Star Wars* movie.

Dystopian Worlds

A dystopia is an anti-utopia. The best dystopian novels use a darker world to reveal truths about our own world. Teens love to read about the worlds and situations that dystopian authors create for their protagonists. So many of the most pressing issues we face as a society, and indeed as a species, are examined in these stories. Ethical or life-and-death struggles around biomedical advances, reproduction control, personal responsibility, disparities in social class, environmental deterioration, overpopulation, and overzealous government control of personal freedoms are all fodder for this genre. Each of the titles highlighted here is an exemplar of a different type of dystopia.

CORE TITLE

★*The Hunger Games,* by Suzanne Collins (BBYA, QP, TTT 2009; PPYA 2011)

Katniss lives in District 12, the poorest of the dozen districts that comprise Panem. Every year, one girl and one boy from each district are chosen by lottery to fight to the death in the televised Hunger Games. Katniss fights in place of her younger sister, and refuses to turn against her opponents for the game's sake. She stands up for the neglected people of her district, and grows into her strength and destiny. She is one in a million, and millions of readers want to be as brave as Katniss. Panem echoes our world in disturbingly obvious ways, from the wealthy one percent to the obsession with reality TV. A love triangle involving two irresistible boys is also crucial to the book's appeal. For those who only know the first book (or movie), it is important to understand how bleak the trilogy becomes. There is no fairy-tale ending. Katniss's fight takes a huge toll on her and on everyone she loves. Even more, she feels responsible for those who choose to rebel in her name.

NEXT READS

★*Unwind*, by Neal Shusterman (BBYA, QP Top Ten 2008)

As the result of a Second Civil War (fought over the issue of abortion), a Bill of Life has been passed. Human life is safeguarded from the moment of conception until age 13, but children ages 13 to 18 may be aborted by their parents. Undesirables are unwound into parts that can be reused for transplantation, thus getting rid of difficult teens and providing a source for transplants. Connor has one week left before his parents send him to a harvest camp. He goes on the lam with his friends Risa and Lev (who is a tithe—a tenth child conceived as a donation to be unwound). Hot-button issues abound in this fast-paced, devastating story driven by flesh-and-blood characters. This book is the first in a consistently excellent series, and fans should be pointed to Shusterman's Thunderhead trilogy next.

Little Brother, by Cory Doctorow (BBYA 2009, John W. Campbell Award; PPYA 2011)

Marcus (known online as w1n5t0n, pronounced "Winston") skips school, and is out enjoying San Francisco when he is caught up in a terrorist attack and imprisoned by the Department of Homeland Security. He is interrogated, and undergoes psychological and physical torture before being released. He vows to fight back against the government using his amazing knowledge of technology and his hacking skills. This novel addresses government surveillance, infringement of civil liberties, intellectual freedom, access to information, social justice, and privacy rights. Magically, Doctorow turns an issue-heavy, politics-ridden novel into a well-paced techno-thriller, largely thanks to the appeal of Marcus and his fellow techies. Fans should also be pointed toward *Pirate Cinema*, in which Doctorow again writes about near-future technology, addressing intellectual property, copyright, and filmmaking.

The Handmaid's Tale, by Margaret Atwood (Arthur C. Clarke Award)

Offred is a Handmaid in the near-future society of Gilead. Pollution has caused an epidemic of infertility, so fertile women are forced to become Handmaids and are assigned to a Commander in order to conceive. Offred remembers her husband and daughter, and what it was like to wear clothes of her own choosing and read good books. Now everyone has a role to play. Gilead is a society created to be a utopia (based on the Bible) that turns into a terrible dystopia. The appeal here is in the world-building and Offred's insistently rebellious thoughts. The pace follows day-to-day life, which is tinged with threatening undertones. There is also a romance between Offred and the Commander's chauffeur. This classic has great appeal for older, more sophisticated teen readers. That said, the 2017 television series may be too intense for most teen readers.

Apocalyptic and Post-Apocalyptic Fiction

Apocalyptic and post-apocalyptic stories are set during or after widespread, world-changing events such as a pandemic, war, disaster, or alien invasion. Scott Westerfeld hit the nail on the head when it comes to their appeal: "The system is asking a lot from teenagers and not giving them much respect in return, so it's no wonder that stories about that system exploding, breaking down under its own contradictions, or simply being overrun by zombies are also beloved of teenagers. What is the apocalypse but an everlasting snow day? An excuse to tear up all those college applications, which suddenly aren't going to determine the rest of your life."[5]

CORE TITLE

★*Ship Breaker,* by Paolo Bacigalupi (Printz Award, BBYA Top Ten 2011; Locus YA; NBA Finalist 2010; PPYA 2016)

In a near-future world ravaged by the effects of global warming, Nailer works on the Gulf Coast with a crew that salvages shipwrecks for copper wire. He does hard, dangerous work in the waters to make his quota. After a violent storm, he finds a girl among the wreckage of a fancy clipper ship, the only survivor. Nita claims her people will pay a reward to get her back, but Nailer's drug addict father, Lopez, finds them first. Caught between Lopez and her own people (whose motives are hardly straightforward), Nita is in grave danger. In a world nearly devoid of morality, Nailer risks his life for a girl he's not sure he can trust. This book is excellent in many areas—world-building, character, pacing, and the way it addresses ethical, moral, and philosophical issues without being didactic. Nailer is ethnically diverse (dark-skinned like his mother, but blue-eyed like his father), and much of what appears in the book feels like it could come true in a matter of decades.

NEXT READS

Ashfall, by Mike Mullin (BFYA 2012; PPYA 2016)

A supervolcano at Yellowstone erupts, and Alex's family home in Cedar Rapids, Iowa, is hit by a rock thrown by the volcano and destroyed. Ashfall blocks the sun and brings on an early winter. Alex sets off on skis toward relatives in Illinois. He faces terrible cold, lack of food and water, and constant threats of violence. Wounded and losing strength, he is saved by a girl his own age and her mother. The teenagers brave gangs of cannibals as they continue toward Illinois. This trilogy is bleak, and at times brutally violent. But there is hope and resourcefulness, and the author has researched the science carefully. The relationship between the two teens is genuine and based on much more than attraction. This book is the first in a trilogy.

The 5th Wave, by Rick Yancey (BFYA, QP, TTT 2014; PPYA 2016)

Sixteen-year-old Cassie and her little brother, Sam, survive the first four waves of an alien invasion that is focused on destroying the entire human race. After Sam is taken by the military to a safe location, Cassie watches as her father and other adults are massacred by their supposed protectors. As she races to find and rescue Sam, she's tracked by an alien "silencer" sent to kill her. The book alternates between Cassie and her old high school friend Ben, who has been transformed into a soldier named "Zombie" by military brainwashing. This first book in a trilogy is notable for taking the time for world-building and character development despite its thriller pacing, and it addresses what makes us human in a changed world.

Station Eleven, by Emily St. Mandel

This adult literary novel connects its characters through one man, Arthur Leander, an actor who dies on stage in Toronto while performing *King Lear* the night before a mass flu pandemic begins to spread through North America. Flashbacks to his youth, early career, and marriages introduce the reader to characters who survive, and some who do not. In the aftermath, the story concentrates on a group of actors and musicians traveling through the Great Lakes region, performing Shakespeare and various orchestral works. The survival of the arts in this post-apocalyptic landscape brings the importance of beauty starkly to life. A graphic novel created by one character encapsulates a longing for the past. For teens interested in important literature that is beautifully and engagingly told, this is a great recommendation.

Expanding Readers' Horizons into the Whole Collection

Movies and television can be a helpful shorthand when trying to determine what kind of science fiction a teen enjoys. And, of course, many of these shows are adaptations of science fiction novels.

Movies — Series

Divergent

Teen dystopian. Continues with *Insurgent* and *Allegiant*. Based on novels by Veronica Roth.

The Hunger Games

Teen dystopian. Continues with *Catching Fire, Mockingjay Part 1, Mockingjay Part 2*. Based on novels by Suzanne Collins.

Jurassic Park

Genetic manipulation. Continues with *The Lost World: Jurassic Park* and *Jurassic Park III*. In 2015, *Jurassic World* returned to the park after ten years of successful operation. Based on novels by Michael Crichton.

The Matrix

Virtual reality. Continues with *The Matrix Reloaded* and *The Matrix Revolutions*.

Star Wars

A new generation caught the fever in 2015 thanks to *Part VII—The Force Awakens*.

Movies — Stand-Alones

Avatar

3D action/adventure.

Guardians of the Galaxy
> Comic space adventure. It was continued in 2017 with *Guardians of the Galaxy Vol. 2*.

Interstellar
> Drama/adventure.

The Martian
> Drama. Mars mission gone wrong. Based on Andy Weir's novel.

Minority Report
> Futuristic crime thriller.

Ready Player One
> Virtual reality thriller. Based on the novel by Ernest Cline.

Starship Troopers
> Military science fiction. Based on the novel by Robert Heinlein.

Television

The 100
> Teens return to Earth ninety-seven years after civilization has been destroyed by a nuclear war.

Doctor Who
> SF/mystery/adventure with heavy time and space travel.

The Expanse
> Space opera. Based on James S. A. Corey's series, which begins with *Leviathan Wakes*.

Firefly
> Space opera. Followed by the film *Serenity*.

Mr. Robot
> Crime drama/cyberthriller.

Star Trek
> The original television series ran from 1966 to 1969. The popular 2009 movie reboot starring Chris Pine continues with *Star Trek into Darkness* and *Star Trek Beyond*.

Stranger Things
> SF/horror/mystery thriller.

Recommendations for Readers' Advisory

How should librarians who don't read in the genre of science fiction get their bearings? Hopefully, this chapter has been helpful. But it is important to listen to our patrons. Teens who read within the genre probably hold strong opinions. Getting a teen advisory group or book club talking about whichever fad is currently sweeping them away can be invaluable.

Science fiction readers are independent and may eschew librarian help. Keep buying the new big titles and putting them on display. Be consistent, so readers will know where to look (and who to ask) when they visit the library.

We have all probably read more science fiction than we realize. *The Time Traveler's Wife? Station Eleven? Never Let Me Go?* These adult titles are great suggestions for teens. And consider recommending the classics. Young readers may not know the science fiction works of writers such as Margaret Atwood or Ursula Le Guin.

Crossover between teen and adult readers is strong in this genre. Teens ignore audience labels, and rightly so. *Ready Player One* and *Pure* could just as easily have been published as young adult books. Also, many adult readers of YA books love dystopian and post-apocalyptic titles.

Keeping Up with New and Upcoming Titles

Journals

Booklist's annual August SF/Fantasy/Horror issue includes Top 10 lists.

Locus Magazine covers science fiction, fantasy, and horror, including young adult books. www.locusmag.com/

VOYA (*Voice of Youth Advocates*) publishes an April Best Science Fiction, Fantasy, and Horror list.

Websites

Tor: www.tor.com/

Original fiction, essays, reviews, rereads, and rewatches. Tor Fiction Affliction publishes monthly lists of new fantasy, science fiction, paranormal, and genre-benders.

i09: http://i09.com/

Science fiction, fantasy, futurism, science, and technology. Monthly "Must-Read List of Science Fiction and Fantasy Books."

Awards and Lists

Arthur C. Clarke Award: www.clarkeaward.com/
    For the best science fiction novel published in the United Kingdom.

Aurealis Awards: http://aurealisawards.org/
    For works by Australians. Notable for young adult and children's categories.

Hugo Awards: www.thehugoawards.org/
    Overseen by the World Science Fiction Society. YA publications are eligible in some categories. Includes the John W. Campbell Award for Best New Writer, the winners of which often have teen appeal, such as Cory Doctorow and John Scalzi.

Locus Awards: www.locusmag.com/
    Winners are determined by *Locus Magazine*'s annual readers' poll. Includes a young adult book category.

Nebula Awards: www.sfwa.org/nebula-awards/
    Awards voted by the Science Fiction and Fantasy Writers of America. They include the Andre Norton Award for Young Adult Science Fiction or Fantasy.

The Reading List (RUSA): www.ala.org/rusa/awards/readinglist
    Highlights outstanding genre fiction, and includes a science fiction winner with read-alikes and a shortlist. Titles often have teen appeal.

Print Resources

Danner, Brandy. *Dark Futures: A VOYA Guide to Apocalyptic, Post-Apocalyptic, and Dystopian Books and Media.* Bowie, MD: VOYA, 2012.

Haley, Guy, ed. *Sci-Fi Chronicles: A Visual History of the Galaxy's Greatest Science Fiction.* Richmond Hill, GA: Firefly, 2014.

Herald, Diana Tixier. *Teen Genreflecting 3: A Guide to Reading Interests.* Santa Barbara, CA: Libraries Unlimited, 2011.

Orr, Cynthia, and Diana Tixier Herald, eds. *Genreflecting: A Guide to Popular Reading Interests.* Santa Barbara, CA: Libraries Unlimited, 2013.

Perry, Karin. *Sci Fi on the Fly: A Guide to Science Fiction for Young Adults.* Bowie, MD: VOYA, 2016.

Saricks, Joyce. *The Readers' Advisory Guide to Genre Fiction.* 2nd ed.
Chicago: American Library Association, 2009.

NOTES

1. Arthur C. Clarke, *The Collected Stories of Arthur C. Clarke,* ed. Patrick Nielsen Hayden (New York: Orb, 2000), ix.
2. Joyce G. Saricks, *The Readers' Advisory Guide to Genre Fiction,* 2nd ed. (Chicago: American Library Association, 2009), 245.
3. Jennifer Stubben Hatch, "All about Science Fiction for Teens," *Novelist Plus.*
4. "Sci-Fi," *Publishers Weekly,* last modified March 9, 2015, www.publishersweekly.com/pw/nielsen/xscifi/20150309.html.
5. Scott Westerfeld, "Breaking Down the 'System,'" The Opinion Pages, Room for Debate, *New York Times,* December 26, 2010, www.nytimes.com/roomfordebate/2010/12/26/the-dark-side-of-young-adult-fiction/breaking-down-the-system.

8

Fantasy

Karyn Silverman

Fantasy, in the simplest terms, refers to one of two conditions: stories in which a system of magic exists, or stories that take place in an imaginary world analogous to or earlier in its technological development than our current world. It's an ancient genre; fairy tales, myths, and legends are all effectively fantasy tales. Like those early tales, fantasy tends to populate worlds with archetypal figures and conflicts—gods and monsters, good and evil, love and hate.

For decades, teen readers of fantasy moved from the children's collection directly to the adult shelves, and crossover reading is still common. The parallel phenomena of *Twilight* and *Harry Potter* ushered in a change, to the point where YA fantasy has refined its own subgenres. Today's teenage fantasy readers have never lacked for choice. Trends such as paranormal romance rise and fall, but works classified as fantasy are a constant feature of the YA landscape and are frequent visitors to the bestseller lists. Fantasy overlaps with horror and science fiction in content and readership; as in those genres, the best fantasy uses its imaginary elements to say something deeper about the real world.

Karyn Silverman is the high school librarian and Educational Technology Department chair at LREI, Little Red School House & Elisabeth Irwin High School. She has served on YALSA's Quick Picks and Best Books for Young Adults committees and was a member of the 2009 Printz committee. She has reviewed for *Kirkus Reviews* and *School Library Journal,* and was an editor of *SLJ*'s "Someday My Printz Will Come" blog.

Because the distinguishing characteristic of fantasy as a genre is tied to the world (specifically the existence of magic or of the imaginary world itself) rather than plot, fantasy is both versatile and difficult to define in simple terms. There are general terms that most readers learn to recognize: epic or high fantasy usually means kings, queens, and multiple volumes; gaslamp indicates a Victorian or analogous setting; low fantasy generally means a real-world setting and a simpler magic system. But none of these descriptors is firmly defined, and even within these more accepted terms there's significant variability. Indeed, fantasy can contain almost any genre set in a magic world; romance, mystery, and adventure are the most common genres, since fantasy tends to be old-fashioned in its emphasis on storytelling and plot. The specifics of a given world—high or low fantasy, primary or secondary worlds, the system of magic and power—vary widely, but the most skillful authors create fully realized worlds. Some worlds will require more buy-in from readers, and will deter casual fantasy readers; imaginary flora and fauna, and new geography and species are all elements that help set the stage for the narrative. The demands of world-building lead to the prevalence of multivolume works (from duologies to series with upwards of ten volumes); stand-alone novels are more likely to have a primary (real) world setting, while series titles are more often set in secondary (imaginary) worlds.

In short, as noted in the introduction to 1997's *Encyclopedia of Fantasy*, fantasy is a "fuzzy set: a set which cannot be defined by its boundaries but which *can* be understood through significant examples of what best represents it."[1] It should come as no surprise, then, that the average fantasy reader knows what he or she likes, but may not know how to describe it.

Appeal

Teen readers of fantasy tend to be opinionated, high-consumption readers, although there are also those who don't mind fantastical elements, but would not classify themselves as fans of the genre. Many fantasy readers are more accurately classed as speculative fiction readers, meaning they are equally at home with fantasy and its near sibling, science fiction, and they may not even distinguish between the two, particularly with books marketed at teen readers where the lines often blur. Fantasy readers often also enjoy graphic novels, from Gaiman's groundbreaking *Sandman* to DC and Marvel's superhero universes, which liberally mix and match fantasy and science fiction elements throughout.

The appeal of fantasy, like all speculative fiction, is that it allows room for serious conversations separated from reality; metaphor can be made tangible. But fantasy also provides escapist fun; it's a space for dreams to play out. The "chosen one" trope transforms a nonentity into an entity (who is often magical or beloved by magical creatures); portal fantasies literally move the protagonist to a new (and inevitably more exciting) world. Teens enjoy both the reflection of their own concerns and the ability to lose themselves in other worlds. Fantasy also lends itself particularly well to fan culture—speculation, fan art, and fanfiction all fit well with the magic and the multivolume works, and fan culture in general has been a strong trend for teens in the last decade or so. Despite the stereotype of fantasy as a gendered genre, YA fantasy in particular abounds in strong female characters and readers.

Setting

Setting defines fantasy. All fantasy can be slotted into high or low fantasy, a setting-specific binary. High fantasy describes fantasy set in a secondary (imaginary) world which has an internal logic; medieval-esque and early industrial-era settings predominate, often with a western European flavor where diversity exists through species, not race, as in *The Lord of the Rings*. Low fantasy is set in the recognizable world, most often in the present or recent past, and mixes fantasy elements into an otherwise realistic setting; the worlds of Harry Potter and Percy Jackson are examples that most teen readers will know. Some readers will move between high and low fantasy, while others will have a strong preference.

Pacing

The plotting in high fantasy aimed at teen readers tends to be complex, with adventure and action playing out against larger political machinations. Low fantasy focuses more on character and mood, but the story-centric nature of the genre means that even the most meditative fantasy tends to have a plot that moves.

Tone

Even when the characters crack jokes and humor enlivens the narrative, there's an earnestness underlying the lightness in fantasy novels.

Situations have real stakes, and magic has consequences. The meaning, purpose, or cost of power are frequent motifs.

Characterization

Fantasy is famous for the existence of "chosen ones," characters who are fated or chosen for some special destiny, so it's no surprise that character development is at least nominally important in most works. Fantasy often contains an emotional journey, whether from innocence to knowledge or from weakness to strength. For too long, mainstream fantasy tended towards a default in which characters were white, cis-gender, and heterosexual; recently, this has begun to shift dramatically.

Story/Theme

Fantasy is primarily a genre of storytelling. The lavish settings of classic high fantasy flop without a story to set against the magic. Because the primary characteristics of fantasy are the focus on story and setting (and its incorporation of magic), fantasy is immensely versatile. However, certain themes show up repeatedly, especially in YA fantasy. Identity and romance are common, as is coming of age, which in fantasy often involves a literal assumption of power.

Key Subgenres and Core Titles in Fantasy

Girl Power

Girl power is primarily a YA-specific subset of high fantasy, and dates back to Tamora Pierce's *Alanna* and Robin McKinley's *The Hero and the Crown*.[2] Authors who came of age on these early (and still relevant) books have continued to expand the offerings. These tales mix adventure, political machination, and a strong romantic vein with a distinctly feminist underpinning. Secondary (imaginary) worlds with low technology predominate; the recent comic series *Another Castle* by Andrew Wheeler is a fantastic example of how this genre is now found in all formats. The appeal of these books crosses genders, and they may appeal to non-genre readers as well; romance and identity provide an immediate access point for teen readers. These are books that tell great stories while exploring universal feelings and conditions.

CORE TITLE

Graceling, by Kristin Cashore (BBYA, TTT, Morris Finalist 2009; PPYA 2012; Mythopoeic Award)

In the world of the Seven Kingdoms, some people are graced, meaning they have a specific supernatural skill in a very particular arena, whether mind reading or baking. Katsa, niece of the Middluns king, is graced with the ability to kill and has been her uncle's weapon since age eight. But fierce, commendable Katsa is ruled by compassion; even as she ostensibly carries out her uncle's orders, she works to undermine him. This leads her to rescue the kidnapped father of the Lienid king, setting off a chain of events that leads her, with Prince Po of Lienid, to face an evil king with an immense, possibly deadly grace. Katsa and Po's partnership and eventual relationship is a template for a healthy, balanced romance; readers will swoon over them while appreciating that the romance doesn't overwhelm the book. The simplistic world-building in the book takes a back seat to character development and a swift plot, which makes this an accessible read as well as an empowering one. This book is the first in a trilogy, but it stands alone.

NEXT READS

The Girl of Fire and Thorns, by Rae Carson (BFYA, Morris Finalist 2012)

Carson's trilogy opener tosses all the overdone tropes of fantasy fiction out the window. Brown-skinned, overweight Princess Elisa is utterly uninterested in power or beauty; she'd rather hide in a library and read. The fascinating world she inhabits is vaguely Spanish in feel, with a desert landscape. Early on Elisa is married to a neighboring king, a widower with a child and a lover. Religion plays a large role in the plot; Elena was blessed with a godstone, indicating some great destiny. The first-person narration makes this book approachable and easy to read despite the clearly distinct secondary world, and Elisa's journey from a frightened, scorned, and isolated girl to a powerful leader will resonate for many. As with *Graceling,* the protagonist is initially "just a girl" who rises to become a strong woman.

Throne of Glass, by Sarah Maas (BFYA 2013)

Celaena is an eighteen-year-old assassin who has been sentenced to a life of hard labor in a salt mine, and she is thus an unlikely heroine. She's vain, calculating, and possibly critical to saving the world; the

King of Adarlan has swept through, killing royal families and imprisoning their people, raising dark forces and destroying the world's balance. Celaena has the opportunity to leave the mine to become the King's Champion, which leads her to the heart of intrigue that is both political and magical. The world here has an impressive breadth, and the complex plotting plays out alongside the requisite (but slow-burning) love triangle. Celaena's small size and feminine gender fool her competitors into underestimating her, a potent commentary on how women are often viewed; additionally, she is supported by a warrior queen (in spirit) and a warrior princess. This book will appeal to fantasy fans who want complicated characters and ever-increasing stakes, and who don't mind a significant commitment (six books).

★*Grave Mercy,* by Robin LaFevers (BFYA 2013)

Unusual for the subgenre, this is an alternate history set in what is recognizably medieval Brittany. LaFevers has added a small pantheon, including the Lord of Death, whose abbey takes in girls and trains them to be assassins. Ismae is one of Death's Handmaidens and is assigned to protect Anne of Brittany (a real figure, whose history is slightly altered here) from the ambitions of France, which would like to annex the smaller kingdom. There is explicit addressing of gender and the way women are treated in society—Anne is beset on all sides by conniving men, while Ismae and her friends have all endured hardships specific to their gender. The fantasy elements are smoothly incorporated, and this will appeal to both fans of feminist fantasy and fans of historical fiction. This book is the first in a trilogy, each focused on a different girl.

Political Fantasy

There's a sweeping scope to the narratives here—these are the stories of empires. Fittingly, the settings often contain callbacks or references to ancient real-world empires like Egypt, Greece, and Rome. These stories (which are inevitably serial) raise questions of right and might, frequently showcasing two or more narrators to show multiple sides of the central conflict. The protagonist usually begins innocent or at least self-interested before becoming consumed by the larger political machinations; scheming outweighs spellcasting, and violence is common. Readers wishing to

---

Young adult books with particular appeal for adult readers are designated with a star (★).

engage with big questions and big battles will find much to appreciate in this subgenre.

CORE TITLE

★*An Ember in the Ashes,* by Sabaa Tahir (BFYA 2016)

An original empire with some features reminiscent of ancient Rome provides the backdrop for a truly epic series. Laia, a Scholar slave whose people were defeated hundreds of years ago by the Martials, joins the revolution and finds herself at Blackcliff, where young Martial warriors train. Elias is the son of the Commandant, but is conflicted and looking for escape. Alternating first-person narratives follow their experiences, which eventually twine together. This is a brutal, breathtaking saga (four books are currently planned); the world-building excels, the magical elements are bleak, and the stakes are high: this book is not for the faint of heart, but it is both an engrossing read and a philosophical examination of power, loyalty, and love. The book features a number of teen characters who are struggling with where they fit in the world and with life-or-death choices that will shape their futures and possibly the future of their world; this plus dark but relatively low-key magic make this book young adult fiction's best answer to *Game of Thrones*.

NEXT READS

The Winner's Curse, by Marie Rutkoski (BFYA 2015)

A military empire where everyone, women included, joins the army or bears new soldiers, has defeated a kingdom that values art and knowledge (worth noting: the conquerors are described as the lighter-skinned race, but are not white). Tactically brilliant but conflicted Kestrel, daughter of the General who masterminded the victory, buys a slave (Arin) who (in alternating third-person narration) is revealed to be a significant player in fomenting a rebellion. The appeal here is twofold; Kestrel and Arin both grapple with their legacies and how to use the power they have, a classic coming-of-age motif; and the seemingly impossible love story here will provide readers with plenty of genuine "feels." This trilogy is easily accessible thanks to the slightly simplified dichotomies describing the world, and it grows more complex with each volume in *The Winner's Trilogy*.

Legacy of Kings, by Eleanor Herman

If the CW Television Network made a show about Alexander the Great (à la Mary Queen of Scots and *Reign*), this series would be the source material. The cast, all of whom have their own chapters and plotlines, comprises a racial and ethnic mix of teens: Macedonian Prince Alex, poor best friend Heph, evil half-sister Cynane, peasants Katerina (more than she seems) and Jacob, and Persian princess Zofia. Sexy, steamy, full of crosses and double-crosses and unexpected alliances, this book is epic and soapy. The present-tense narration keeps the pages turning, but the complicated quasi-historical setting makes this most suited to readers who are well-versed in big fantasy sagas and are seeking a new world to explore. This book is the first in a trilogy.

The Name of the Wind, by Patrick Rothfuss (Alex 2008)

If the average political fantasy protagonist starts out self-interested, then Kvothe is above average: a teen prodigy in a secondary world where magic and myth intersect, he's a little bit in love with himself. The political machinations emerge slowly, interwoven with Kvothe's memories of his childhood and university years as well as a present in which he's hiding after (maybe) killing a king. Kvothe is pure adolescence (although the book was published for adults): cocky, consumed by school and friends, and madly in love with a mercurial girl. He's also consumed by his parent's murder at the hands of a power that no one else believes exists. The heavy coming-of-age elements here mean there are fewer big battles, but plenty of small fights. Absorbing and first in a not yet complete trilogy, this book is for readers seeking deep engagement, opportunities to speculate, and precision writing that never falters.

Grimdark

A recently coined term, grimdark describes books that are, well, grim and dark; George R. R. Martin's *A Song of Ice and Fire* (TV's *Game of Thrones*) is the poster child. Grimdark fiction is set in secondary worlds and plays on the classic heroic subgenre of high fantasy (its readership overlaps significantly with political fantasy). Grimdark scoffs at clichéd perfect heroes and instead populates magical worlds with criminals and antiheroes. It's no surprise that teens lap these stories up, especially those who feel out of step with adult expectations; imperfect heroes prove that you can be great even when you aren't necessarily being good. While grimdark elements are beginning to populate YA books, it's a subgenre mostly found on the adult shelves; three of the four books below are crossover rather than YA.

CORE TITLE

★*Six of Crows*, by Leigh Bardugo (BFYA, TTT 2016)

Set in the same world as Bardugo's *Grisha* trilogy of political fantasy novels, this is an ensemble tale of racially diverse, streetwise teens who take on the corrupt establishment, led by emotionally and physically scarred Kaz. The cast is archetypal, but also painfully real despite the fantasy setting (a nineteenth-century analogue of Amsterdam); one teen has clear learning issues, and another has a gambling addiction that endangers his family's security; several are scarred from horrific past experiences—Inez, who along with Kaz centers the narrative, was forced into the sex trade after slavers kidnapped her. In short, there's someone here for everyone, and the admittedly fantastic struggles provide pulse-pounding action and the opportunity to witness how broken but beautiful people can make a difference, which resonates strongly with teen readers. Bardugo throws in romance (gay and straight), secrets, serious issues, and some fantastic machinations. As long as they can handle the darkness (although there's humor, too), readers will want the second volume of the duology the moment they finish the first.

NEXT READS

A Darker Shade of Magic, by Victoria Schwab

Adopted Kell suspects that the royal family of Antares, the capital of magical Red London, only wants him for his power: as an Antari, Kell has the ability to traverse across the three Londons. Kell's rebellion, which involves smuggling items between the Londons, opens his world to an ancient threat. The street thief Lila is a (Gray London) thief who follows Kell into Red London. The characters are young adults chafing against their worlds, and the writing is evocative. While readers may ship Kell and Lila, this book is largely romance-free; familial relationships (in many cases absent or destructive ones) play a much larger role in it, making this an excellent recommendation for teens who would rather never see another love triangle.[3] While technically an adult title from Schwab, who also writes YA, only the price point gives it away. This book is the first in a trilogy.

The Lies of Locke Lamora, by Scott Lynch (BBYA 2007)

Best described as *Game of Thrones* meets *Ocean's Eleven,*[4] this adult title has immense teen appeal. Lynch's Venice-inspired Camorr is full of thieves and killers, chief among them Locke Lamora and his gang called the Gentleman Bastards, the most famed criminals in Camorr—although not even their Capa (or mob boss) knows it. The story takes an abrupt twist from fun to dark around the midpoint, and Locke and his best friend end up toe to toe with a truly threatening figure who wields unpleasant magical powers; meanwhile, they need to pull off a long con of immense complexity to stop their foe. This book is profane, funny, dark, and utterly delicious, and it is a classic example of grimdark. The narrative cuts back and forth to Locke's (very brutal) childhood, amping up the book's already unmistakable appeal factor for younger readers. The book is a series opener, but it stands alone.

A Game of Thrones, by George R. R. Martin (Locus Award)

It seems slightly redundant to list this book here, given that this (still unfinished, perpetually best-selling) series has introduced gritty, sweeping, political fantasy to so many readers, but in fact many of them know the show rather than the books, and the two diverge widely. The complex plot in short: even as the Seven Kingdoms are torn by a war of succession, pitting families against each other (including a number of teen characters), a magical threat is rising behind the massive, ancient protective wall. The book's chapters switch perspective regularly, with the reader only knowing what the characters know, which means that surprises lie everywhere, many of them brutal. This is clearly an adult title, with sex and sexual violence, but older teen readers will lap it up; the name brand recognition doesn't hurt either.

Mythopoeic Fantasy

If fantasy is ultimately about story, and stories are often about moments of change and transformation, then mythopoeic fantasy may be the quintessential fantasy genre. As defined by the Mythopoeic Society, it "creates a new and transformative mythology, or incorporates and transforms existing mythological material."[5] Although the mythopoeic tradition grew out of the works of J. R. R. Tolkien, this subgenre is not all high fantasy; in young adult literature, contemporary low fantasies with strong mythic elements, like 2016 Printz winner *Bone Gap,* predominate. These are fantasies that awaken a sense of wonder and feel real, tapping into archetypal elements and universal emotions.

CORE TITLE

★*The Raven Boys,* by Maggie Stiefvater (BFYA, TTT 2013)

Blue, the daughter of a psychic in a small southern town, hates the rich boys at Aglionby Academy on principle. But when she uses her strange power (she isn't psychic, but amplifies others) to help her aunt see the names of those who will die in the next year, she sees an Aglionby boy. Which means either she's his true love or the reason for his death; and given the prophecy that her kiss will kill her true love, she is possibly both. What follows is a quartet of books about Blue and her raven boys, four Aglionby students, each uncanny and wonderful in different ways. Stiefvater draws on Welsh mythology and creates her own magical counter-reality, but she also tells a powerful story of friendship. Blue, Gansey, Adam, Ronan, and Noah's experiences are transfigurative for them and are also powerfully affecting for readers. They contend with family complications, class and financial realities, and threats supernatural and mundane. The general mood is less action and more exploration, with gorgeous writing.

NEXT READS

Guardian of the Dead, by Karen Healey (BBYA, Morris Finalist 2011, PPYA 2013, Aurealis Award)

Awkward, prickly Ellie is an outcast in her New Zealand boarding school, with an impressive track record of rule-breaking. Her desire to stay out of trouble falls apart when she drunkenly agrees to take part in a play, through which she becomes embroiled in a mystery centered around attractive Mark and possibly involving a series of gruesome murders. Mark and the murders are eventually revealed to have something to do with the Maori "fairy folk," the patupaiarehe. References to Shakespeare and Greek mythology resonate through this book, which is a fantasy mystery steeped in New Zealand's history and culture, and which simultaneously explores race, appropriation, body image, and identity. Ellie and her friends (glamorous Iris, asexual Kevin, and possibly not human Mark) are engaging and raw; and their evolving relationships are as compelling as the magic.

Alif the Unseen, by G. Willow Wilson (World Fantasy Award)

This adult crossover novel, written by the same author as the more recent *Ms. Marvel* comic series, explores Middle Eastern mythology and technology. The Arab-Indian hacker Alif has just been dumped by the wealthy young woman of his dreams, and he's been hacked himself, by the head of the (unnamed) state security service. He stumbles onto a book of jinn (genies) and into an adventure that seamlessly blends magic and technology. This is an adult title, but teens will love young hacker Alif, who is scarcely past his own teen years, and be entranced by sarcastic, ancient Vikram, a jinn of unimaginable power and almost as much attitude. Like *Mr. Penumbra's 24-Hour Bookstore*, another popular crossover, this is an adventure puzzle that uses old ideas to tell a thoroughly modern story.

American Gods, by Neil Gaiman (Hugo, Nebula, Locus, Bram Stoker Awards)

This modern classic (now a TV series) is an adult title by an author already well loved by teen readers, making it an ideal crossover. Racially indeterminate Shadow is released early from jail after his wife and best friend die in a car accident, an event that destroys everything Shadow lived for and believed in. He is hired by Mr. Wednesday, and they set off on a surreal road trip that brings together old gods and new. History, immigration, and identity roil together in Shadow's journey. This is a smart, literate, twisty book that is designed to make the reader think. Teens will love the subtle, dark humor and the way Gaiman reinvents everything; through his eyes, the modern world becomes a fascinating place of mystery. While this book stands alone, there is a much lighter companion, *Anansi Boys*.

Fairy Tale Retellings

Retellings focus on archetypal stories made fresh; and retellings, which range from classic tales, legends, and myths to modern fairy tales like *The Wizard of Oz*, never go out of style. Retellings for teens are often grimmer than those for children, allowing readers to immerse themselves in the familiar while also exploring new territory; it's the remix culture of teen lives played out in literature. As in the source material, the protagonists of these books often experience a journey through the wilderness (literal or figurative) with little adult support, in line with the adolescent shift to a peer-focused existence. Some retellings, like the graphic novel series *Fables,* mash the characters into new genres (volume one is distinctly noir in tone); others, like *Ash,* maintain more of a classic feeling.

CORE TITLE

Ash, by Malinda Lo (Morris Finalist 2009, PPYA 2014)

In a classic fairy tale land—vaguely medieval, with a magical forest and fairies—Aisling (Ash) is a daughter who loses her mother to death and her father to his new wife and stepdaughters even before he dies. This book starts as a riff on the familiar Cinderella tale, reinvented by Lo as a story of grief and finally as a love affair not with a prince but with his Huntress Kaisa. Ash is a nature lover, a quiet girl whose love of fairy stories and grief lead her into danger when she bargains with Sidhean, who is far from the traditional fairy godmother. In the end, as in so many fairy tales, this is a story about love as power, and, like love, it manages to feel fresh and new even though it's built on very old bones. Lo has also written a prequel, *Huntress,* which incorporates Chinese mythology and the *I Ching.*

NEXT READS

Vassa in the Night, by Sarah Porter (BFYA 2017)

Vassilissa the Brave, one of Russia's best-known fairy tales, transitions unexpectedly well to contemporary Brooklyn. Orphaned Vassa lives with her complex family, which consists of three sisters, one black, one white, and one biracial, not all related by blood, who are being raised by Vassa's father's abandoned wife. They live in the kind of Brooklyn neighborhood that tourists don't visit. When Vassa enters the witch Baba Yaga's bodega, which almost no one leaves alive, she and the sociopathic talking doll her mother left her find themselves fighting to outwit the witch. Vassa's narration is fully contemporary even as the story sometimes seems timeless. Teens who love horror will love this—Baba Yaga is a very wicked witch—but the fairy tale elements are even more prevalent, from the gorgeous writing to the magic that pervades and shapes everything.

A Thousand Nights, by E. K. Johnston

This is a retelling of the *1,001 Nights* frame story, gorgeously told by a nameless narrator, a Middle Eastern girl in an ancient polytheistic world. The king here is Lo-Melkhiin, a djinn (although never named as such) who has killed 300 girls before the narrator marries him to save her beloved sister. It's easy to rave about the stylistic accomplishment of this book, but there is also substance; the resourceful, kind, and brave narrator pushes back, using the small magics of women—spinning yarn, spinning stories—against Lo-Melkhiin, even as her family deify her as a household god and unknowingly use their prayers to bolster her power. This is a dreamy, thoughtful, lush, and feminist retelling that manages to respect the source while using it to say something new. This book is perfect for readers who are looking for something unusual.

Witches Abroad, by Terry Pratchett

Terry Pratchett is a genre unto himself, particularly the *Discworld* series. This subseries about witches specifically focuses on retelling tales, using them for satiric commentary (his specialty) and as the bones of original tales. *Witches Abroad* shakes up several fairy tales and the fairy godmother motif in particular; a fairy godmother dies, leaving her heir stuck trying to figure out how it all works and pitting her and her allies against another fairy godmother who uses magic mirrors and has turned to the dark. Many teens already know Pratchett from his children's titles; this book is an accessible introduction to his sharper adult work. It will appeal to readers interested in the why of fairy tales rather than the content, and who like retellings focused on examining underlying assumptions about society, gender, and good and evil.

Fantastic Beasts

It is no surprise, in a genre full of both magical creatures and teens figuring themselves out, that some teens turn out to be not actually human. This perfect metaphor for adolescence allows a rich exploration of questions of identity, wrapped up in magical worlds where humanity is more about *how* you are than *who* you are, a theme resonant for teen readers. This is a subgenre focused on character first, but not at the expense of setting or plot.

CORE TITLE

Daughter of Smoke and Bone, by Laini Taylor (BFYA 2012)

Blue-haired Karou is an art student in Prague. Her notebooks are filled with sketches of teeth and strange creatures; not even her best friend, the fierce, funny, and tiny Zuzanna, knows that these are not imaginary scenes. Karou has a secret existence; behind a door only she can open, there is a shop where strange creatures sell wishes, and this is Karou's family. When a flaming angel appears in Prague just as Karou's family vanishes, she learns that there is more to everything; she is actually a Chimera from another world, and the Seraph, to whom she feels a strange attraction even as his people try to kill hers, holds answers to her past. Karou is spunky and funny; she and Zuzanna could hold their own even in a less inventive setting, but happily the immense mythology that Karou comes from is equally strong. Who Karou really is, what she values, and how that will change the world unfolds over three volumes, each one better than the last.

NEXT READS

Seraphina, by Rachel Hartman (BFYA, Morris Award, Horn Book Honor 2013)

In a secondary world most reminiscent of the High Renaissance, dragons who can take a human form but are nevertheless immensely inhuman are reluctant allies. The musician Seraphina has spent her life hiding her half-dragon heritage (revealed midway in the book), but when she accepts a position as assistant to the court composer on the same day Prince Rufus is murdered, possibly by renegade dragons, she finds herself in the heart of everything. This is a mystery that explores prejudice and identity. Seraphina's dry, prickly voice will appeal to intellectual readers; Hartman's dragons are original and serve as metaphors for almost anything that alienates, but they are also vibrant, individual characters. The strong emphasis on music in the book adds an additional hook for readers. Although there is a sequel, this book stands alone.

The Replacement, by Brenna Yovanoff (BFYA 2011)

Somewhere in middle America, in a town called Gentry, it's not uncommon for human babies to be taken, and fairy changelings left in their place in the cribs. Most of these changelings, or replacements, quickly sicken and die. Mackie is a replacement. He's lasted sixteen years, trying to pass for normal in a world that hurts him: he is allergic to iron, blood, and consecrated ground—even the strings of his beloved bass hurt. The idea of feeling like you don't fit in is made brutally real here, and is combined with a beautiful, sometimes horrific new riff on the changeling legend. Mackie's withdrawal from the world is both actual and a metaphor for depression; his willingness to fight the magic underground for a classmate's taken sister is about reclaiming his own life. The writing is beautiful, and the characters are average (extra)ordinary teens. This book will appeal to fans of mythopoeic fantasy and fairy tale retellings, as well as horror and mystery fans.

Uprooted, by Naomi Novik (Nebula Award, Mythopoeic Award)

In a secondary world based on the Poland of fairy tales and legends, there is a dragon in the woods who steals a beautiful young woman every ten years. But the dragon is actually a crotchety (but not unattractive) wizard, and the girl he chooses is stubborn, contrary Agnieszka. There's a best friend turned to wood, a rising magical threat, a great deal of misunderstanding, and a romance that feels old-fashioned and cozy: it sounds like a lot, but Novik's lovely writing pulls it all together. Agnieszka's immense power blossoms with her confidence and understanding, and she herself is a classic adolescent, moving from rebellion and relatively limited power to become a strong woman. This stand-alone adult novel will appeal to readers looking for fairy tales, mythopoeic fantasy, love stories, and tales of power and transformation.

Urban Fantasy

Urban fantasy is defined by its setting, which must be some sort of city. While urban fantasy is not exclusively a low fantasy subgenre, most readers will assume and prefer a contemporary, real-world locale, though one with fantastic intrusions. (For the rare reader who wants an urban secondary world setting, you should suggest the incomparable Terry Pratchett's *City Watch* books.) The city setting means these books are often gritty, and sometimes (as with *Shadowshaper*) they appeal to readers who prefer realistic urban fiction. Paranormal romance is urban fantasy that focuses on human/nonhuman romantic entanglements; some readers won't distinguish between the two, but some will want the grit without too many kisses.[6]

CORE TITLE

City of Bones, by Cassandra Clare (PPYA 2011)

The book that launched a thousand sequels (and counting) and inspired massive fan engagement, *City of Bones* is a quintessential urban fantasy, in which humans and downworlders battle. The main character and everygirl Clary finds herself drawn into mystery, danger, and a forbidden romance after she witnesses three teens kill a demon; it turns out Clary is a Shadowhunter, and she joins forces with the other Shadowhunters to fight darkness. Rife with action, a new mythology, and romantic entanglements, it's easy to see why this book is so popular, and Clare uses the "chosen one" trope to good effect with outsider Clary. The book's appeal lies in a motley cast of appealing characters who spar with words and bodies, an ever-expanding mythology, and a downright cinematic flair for description; no wonder a movie and TV series have both followed. Connected works in Clare's universe expand the world in time and locale and introduce additional characters, including LGBTQ and racially diverse teens; in other words, every reader can find herself in Clare's still-growing world.

NEXT READS

Tithe, by Holly Black (BBYA, TTT 2003)

This book's setting is technically suburban, but the grit—broken glass-filled streams, angry teens in a dead-end world, neglectful parents—makes this "modern faerie tale" a perfect urban fantasy read-alike. Sixteen-year-old Kaye is back in New Jersey, where she used to see faeries, when she comes across a handsome inhuman knight; in saving him, she draws herself into the intrigue between warring courts. Black's faeries are cruel and beautiful, and magical without kindness; human-raised Kaye is no angel herself (she drinks, steals, and half-accidentally enchants her best friend's boyfriend), but she's an admirable antihero who will resonate for anyone who feels out of place and longs for magic. Black doesn't shy away from unpleasantness, killing off characters and leaving things uncertain, and she doesn't shy away from sexiness either. Despite being older than many of today's teens, this book—which introduced a mythos that Black is still adding to—has lost none of its ugly-beautiful appeal.

Shadowshaper, by Daniel José Older (BFYA, QP Top Ten 2016)

Brooklyn girl and graffiti artist Sierra Santiago likes to hang out with her friends in their rapidly gentrifying neighborhood. She's a normal girl in a normal world, until paintings start crying and corpses start walking. It turns out that Sierra, like her grandparents, is a shadow-shaper, and someone wants them all dead. The novel weaves magic into the multicultural melting pot that is Brooklyn; Sierra needs to harness her magic in order to save herself, and the threats to her neighborhood may be part of the puzzle as well. The standout is not the magic (fascinating as it is), but the vibrant, realistic teen characters and their complex relationships with each other and their changing neighborhood. This is as urban as fantasy gets, and urban teens will love seeing themselves and their world in a compulsively readable magical tale.

Sunshine, by Robin McKinley (BBYA 2005, Mythopoeic Award)

Set in a slightly alternate present, this adult novel manages to provide much of what readers love in urban fantasy: paranormal creatures (specifically vampires), danger, and an absorbing first-person narrator. However, this is urban fantasy as written by Robin McKinley, who tends to include minutiae and romance in equal doses and always tells a bigger story. Sunshine works in her family's bakery after barely graduating from high school; she finds herself kidnapped by a set of vampires, and ends up in a magical feud allied with a terrifying yet alluring vampire. Sunshine herself, who is in her twenties and trying to find her place, is ferocious but not brave, and she will provide teen readers with a kind of mirror, although her battles are with the undead as well as with familial expectations. Humor and warmth meld with genuinely scary vampires and a fascinating world, making this an unusual but compulsively readable take on paranormal romance.

Historical Fantasy

Whether set against actual history with magic added, or in an alternate time line in which magic has always existed, historical fantasy derives much of its charm from riffing on the known. Setting usually plays a significant role, while major world history events, which often form a critical backdrop in realistic historical fiction, are less important here than the mores, costumes, and limitations of the period (commonly the eighteenth to twentieth centuries). There is significant overlap with steampunk science fiction in this subgenre's readership, and the characters tend to be iconoclasts and rule-breakers who appeal to readers who want their magic mixed with social concerns and lavish set pieces.

CORE TITLE

Chime, by Franny Billingsley (BFYA, AAYA 2012; NBA finalist 2011; PPYA 2016)

The rapidly changing world of the 1920s provides a historical setting that Billingsley uses to great effect. In industrialized London there are motorcars and electric lights; but in the Swampsea (based on the British Fens), time moves more slowly and the Old Ones still exert a presence. Briony, who narrates in a thoroughly original voice, communicates with the Old Ones and believes herself to be a witch who is responsible for fires, floods, and injuries. Change—the changing world, and Briony's changing perception of her own experiences—provides the thematic anchor here. The unreliable narration makes it difficult for readers to immediately discern real from imaginary magic, and for much of the novel it obscures the truth of Briony's past abuse (emotional and magical) at the hands of her stepmother. Briony would like to learn and to run wild in the Swamp, to write stories and live and love freely, but instead she's expected to behave nicely, dress properly, and care for the household and her disabled twin, making this an exploration of society and feminism as well as brilliant storytelling.

NEXT READS

★*The Dark Days Club,* by Alison Goodman

A Regency romance with demons? Think Georgette Heyer but fantasy, and you'll have a sense of this impeccably researched fantasy novel that tackles feminism, freedom, sexuality, demons, and a slow-burning but hot romance. Lady Helen is eighteen and wants to be a good girl—but she's developing uncommon strength and starting to see strange things, because she's a Reclaimer, one of a handful who can vanquish the demons that feed on people's emotions. The usual conflicts—family tension, attraction to the wrong type of man (he has an unsavory reputation)—are heightened by the otherworldly stakes. There's a gentle sense of fun mixed with provocative questions, and serious fantasy readers who don't like sword-and-sorcery tales will find this a better fit; it marries the powerful protagonists of the "girl power" stories with a more realistic and personal sense of the world. This is the first book in a trilogy.

★*Dreamhunter,* by Elizabeth Knox (BBYA 2007)

Set in the early twentieth century in Southland, a fantasy analogue of New Zealand, this is a family story that centers on political corruption and the fight to do the right thing even when it's neither easy nor convenient. In Southland some people can catch dreams, which they can then share out, and this power has rapidly become critical to Southland's economy. Laura Hame and Rose Tiebold, teen cousins at the center of the duology, are not always likable, but their struggle to define themselves against their famous families will be familiar to teen readers. Knox evokes a past when societal expectations shaped the lives of young women, and balances her historical sense with an original magic system and a fierce social conscience. Another book by Knox, *Mortal Fire,* set in the 1950s, further explores the complex magic and race and class tensions of Southland.

The Night Circus, by Erin Morgenstern (Alex 2012, Locus Award)

At the turn of the last century, two magicians play a game: one apprentice against the other, in a magical competition that can only end with death. The playing field is a circus, Le Cirque des Rêves, an extraordinary space where dreams become reality. The prose here is evocative and moody, and the lush descriptive writing takes center stage, subsuming the fairly slight plot (the competition, the growing love, and the way that Celia and Marco defy the adults who control them). This book is beautifully written, with a melancholy love story at the center and two appealing but distant protagonists and a host of more accessible hangers-on. It is the kind of book that invites fan art and word of mouth; dreamy romantics will flock to it.

Expanding Readers' Horizons into the Whole Collection

When determining readers' taste in fantasy, movies, television, games, and graphic novels provide clues. Fantasy readers often enjoy the multimedia DC and Marvel universes, including television and movie properties, and should be pointed to those as well as the specific titles listed below.

Movies

Fantastic Beasts and Where to Find Them

Historical fantasy. Part of J. K. Rowling's Wizarding World, the first not based on a book.

Labyrinth

(Sub)urban fantasy/fairy tale retelling.

The Lord of the Rings
> Based on the novels by J. R. R. Tolkien.

The Princess Bride
> Quasi-historical, comedic, romantic fantasy.

Stardust
> Mythopoeic. Based on the novel by Neil Gaiman.

Television

American Gods
> Mythopoeic fantasy. Based on the novel by Neil Gaiman. Adult content.

Game of Thrones
> Grimdark, political fantasy. Based on the series by George R. R. Martin. Adult content.

The Magicians
> Based on the series by Lev Grossman. Adult content.

Once Upon a Time
> Fairy tale retelling meets urban fantasy.

Reign
> Historical fantasy.

Games and Apps

There are numerous fantasy-themed board and video games, which many teens will already know. Below are a few of the most notable.

Dungeons and Dragons
> High fantasy role-playing game (analog). A great candidate for a library program.

Final Fantasy
> Political and epic fantasy video game. First in a multi-platform franchise.

The Legend of Zelda
> High fantasy action and puzzle video game. First in a multi-platform franchise.

Recommendations for Readers' Advisory

The first step in supporting fantasy readers is to respect their taste. The sidelined geeks of the 1980s have become creators of movies, television shows, and books, bringing the previously peripheral into the mainstream, but adults who work with teens sometimes still act as if fantasy is less respectable because it isn't realistic.

It's also critical to know what's coming up; the newest book is often the best suggestion for the reader who may have already read the whole fantasy section in the library. Knowing when the newest book in a beloved series is coming, and making sure the shelves are stocked with the complete runs of series titles will serve most readers well and will build a sense of trust.

Because fantasy can encompass any genre while not being subject to the limitations of the real world, it offers something for nearly every reader, even those who believe they don't like fantasy. More and more fantasy-influenced titles are appearing in "literary" lists (look for keywords like "magic realism") and in romance; these titles will appeal widely, whereas high fantasy generally has a more specific readership. The lighter fantasy elements in magic realism and romance also provide an entry point for the librarian who doesn't usually read the genre, although it's only one subset of fantasy. Finally, as fantasy readers tend to read above and below their reading level, upper middle grade and adult fantasy should also be freely recommended to teen readers.

Keeping Up with New and Upcoming Titles

Journals

Booklist's annual August SF/Fantasy/Horror issue includes Top 10 lists.

Locus Magazine covers science fiction, fantasy, and horror, including young adult books. www.locusmag.com/

VOYA (Voice of Youth Advocates) publishes an April Best Science Fiction, Fantasy, and Horror list.

Kirkus Reviews frequently features science fiction and fantasy in online articles and blog posts. http://kirkusreviews.com.

Websites

Book Smugglers: http://thebooksmugglers.com/

Blog turned independent publisher, featuring original stories and book reviews, primarily fantasy, with particular attention paid to issues of diversity and representation.

Tor: www.tor.com/

Original stories, essays, reviews, rereads, and rewatches focused on speculative fiction. Monthly Fiction Affliction list of new fantasy, science fiction, paranormal, and genre-benders is a good source of what's new.

Unbound Worlds: www.unboundworlds.com/

Affiliated with Penguin Random House, but not publisher-exclusive. Especially noteworthy are the new release lists (including graphic novels and games) and Cage Match, an annual feature that will engage teen fans with the larger fan community.

Awards and Lists

Aurealis Awards: http://aurealisawards.org/

For works by Australians. Notable for young adult and children's categories.

Hugo Awards: www.thehugoawards.org/

Overseen by the World Science Fiction Society, but includes fantasy and horror titles. Winners often have teen appeal, and teen titles are occasionally recognized.

Locus Awards: www.locusmag.com/

Winners are determined by *Locus Magazine*'s annual readers' poll. Includes a Best Fantasy Novel category; featured titles generally have teen appeal. The young adult book category winners are usually fantasy.

Mythopoeic Awards: www.mythsoc.org/awards.htm

Administered by the Mythopoeic Society. Adult and children's awards are given each year; books with teen appeal crop up on both award lists.

Nebula Awards: www.sfwa.org/nebula-awards/
> Voted by the Science Fiction and Fantasy Writers of America. Includes the Andre Norton Award for Young Adult Science Fiction or Fantasy.

World Fantasy Awards: www.worldfantasy.org/
> Administered by the World Fantasy Convention, with annual awards in ten categories. Nominated novels often have teen appeal and are sometimes teen titles.

Print Resources

Herald, Diana Tixier. *Teen Genreflecting 3: A Guide to Reading Interests.* 2011.

Orr, Cynthia, and Diana Tixier Herald, eds. *Genreflecting: A Guide to Popular Reading Interests.* 2013.

Saricks, Joyce. *The Readers' Advisory Guide to Genre Fiction.* 2009.

NOTES

1. John Clute and John Grant, *The Encyclopedia of Fantasy* (New York: St. Martin's, 1997). While this is now out of print, the text (which is dated but still worth perusing) can be browsed online at http://sf-encyclopedia.uk.
2. Bonnie Kunzel and Susan Fichtelberg, *Tamora Pierce* (Westport, CT: Greenwood, 2007).
3. "Ship," short for relationship, is a term from fanfiction. To "ship" something is to be a fan of the relationship, which may or may not actually exist in the text. "I really ship Romeo and Rosalind, and I don't see why he went for Juliet, that's what caused all the trouble," is a usage example no teen would ever actually use, but it gives a sense of the grammatical use.
4. This is the comparison I've used for years, and many reviewers make the same comparison. The earliest incidence of it seems to be the Agony Column review quoted on Scott Lynch's website: www.scottlynch.us/books.html.
5. Edith Crowe, "About the Society," The Mythopoeic Society, www.mythsoc.org/about.htm.
6. For a more detailed description of YA urban fantasy and particularly how it differs from adult urban fantasy (which tends to have a lot of sex and violence), see http://stackedbooks.org/2015/02/get-genrefied-ya-urban-fantasy.html.

9

Horror

Horror has always been popular with young adult readers. From ghost stories around a campfire to screaming along with friends at the movies, its popularity is nearly a cliché. The books of R. L. Stine, Lois Duncan, and Christopher Pike have been handed to many a reluctant reader, and Stephen King's many best-selling horror novels are a proven gateway for teens who are ravenous for a good story.

For the purposes of this chapter, horror is defined as fiction that intends to scare its readers. It is a genre that inspires emotion, rather than intellectual puzzling.[1] Horror deals in dread, menace, terror, gore, violence, and foreboding. In other words, it is not the shiver-tinged romance of *Twilight* or the dark fantasy of Cassandra Clare, or even the dystopian warfare of Patrick Ness's *Chaos Walking* series. While those series include elements of horror, their primary appeal lies elsewhere.

Paranormal elements have leaked into every genre, including that of horror. Some teens consider Maggie Stiefvater's *Shiver* to be horror, in which case we need to change tack and begin thinking about paranormal romance to recommend. But pure horror, a literature meant to inspire terror and dread, does exist in teen literature. In fact, at the time of this writing, horror is experiencing a renaissance in popular culture. Consider television series, both original (*American Horror Story, Supernatural*) and adaptations (*Under the Dome, The Vampire Diaries*), movies too numerous to mention, and popular graphic novel series (*The Walking Dead, Locke & Key*).

Most YA horror includes an element of the supernatural, and often a monster of some kind. Rick Yancey's *Monstrumologist* series includes both actual monsters and a monstrous human, a scientist so engrossed in his work that he neglects his young apprentice. Many teen horror novels mix the supernatural with a threat of *this* world—a serial killer, the challenge of post-apocalyptic survival, a pandemic or natural disaster. Some would put serial killers in this chapter, but in this book they live in the "Thrillers" chapter.

Given that we are focused on teen readers, it will come as no surprise that the best horror novelists integrate themes that will interest their target age group. YA horror novels include plenty of foreboding and gore, but they also address identity, ethical questions (i.e., do zombies have souls?), and coming-of-age touchstones. Teen horror addresses dark issues, such as racism, bullying, homophobia, and abuse. Teens are often heroes in these novels on account of their making tough choices or taking action in impossible situations, with little or no time to think and no adult guidance.

A thorough readers' advisory interview is crucial when finding books for a teen seeking horror. Teens, just like adults, have varying comfort levels with violence and gore. Teens expect to be grossed out, but just how much blood they can handle depends on the individual teen. Horror is personal. What scares one fifteen-year-old boy may cause another to just laugh. And there is a big difference between the psychological creepiness of Adele Griffin's *Tighter* and the disorienting terror of Andrew Smith's *The Marbury Lens*.

Appeal

Reading horror is pure escapism. The emotions generated by a terrific horror novel can eclipse even the worst day at school. We read horror to distract us from real life, or to experience the thrill of living close to the edge. Readers get hooked on the intensity of these stories.

Horror has long been considered beneath literary readers, and this mainstream rejection may be part of what drives rebellious teens to dive right in. But mostly they seek the adrenaline rush, the physical immediacy of the fear deep in their gut. At the same time, it is the joy of the safe scare—feeling terrified while safely at home or hanging out with friends in front of the television set.

There are generally considered to be two types of horror, storyteller and visceral.[2] In the first, the creepy elements of the story build gradually, usually within a familiar setting: a small town, or the corridors of a high school. In visceral novels, the terror begins immediately and never lets up. Robin Wasserman's *The Waking Dark,* for example, begins with multiple, simultaneous brutal murders in one small town.

Setting

Setting is the groundwork upon which all the other elements depend. It may be dark and isolated, unfamiliar, or the familiar that has been unexpectedly altered. Regardless, the author finds a way to communicate that something is off, and is just wrong enough to make the reader feel uneasy.

Tone

Horror authors find inventive ways of establishing the mood and tone of their story. *Miss Peregrine's Home for Peculiar Children* uses creepy old photographs. The endpapers of Rick Yancey's *Monstrumologist* series display anatomical drawings of monsters' body parts.

Language is the most obvious way that authors establish tone. The languid, description-rich beginning to a gothic historical setting conveys a different expectation than a dialogue-heavy action scene launching a zombie thriller. Some authors purposefully create distance from the horror of the story, while others throw it right in the reader's face. Either way, vivid and precise language is key.

Pacing

In the storytelling horror novel, the author carefully controls the level of foreboding, orchestrating a gradual acceleration into terror. Storylines can be unpredictable, and surprising twists and jolts keep the reader on edge. Gore ratchets up bit by bit, allowing readers to tolerate more violence by the end of a novel than they would at the beginning.[3] Visceral horror novels give readers less time to catch their breath and provide more frequent jolts, and that is what their fans expect.

Characterization

The protagonists in YA horror novels are almost always teens, often troubled but likeable. They may be vulnerable outsiders, underdogs who find an unexpected inner strength when called upon to face a monster or monstrous situation.[4] They may have done or said something they are ashamed of, or they are hiding something, or are embarrassed by their outsider status, which puts them off balance from the start.

Story/Theme

Many horror protagonists tell their own story, which lends immediacy to the narrative. They may use humor as a defense mechanism, which helps to lighten the tone. Most narrators are sympathetic. The reader is meant to care about them from the first pages. In any case, point of view is critical. The reader rarely sees the story from the villain's point of view, which increases the likelihood of surprise and terror.[5]

Key Subgenres and Core Titles in Horror

Monsters

Who doesn't love a good monster? And by "monster," I mean an evil, terrifying creature that threatens our very sanity with its existence. Supernatural creatures are fascinating, and very scary because they are unpredictable. They are not part of our everyday world. We call some people monsters (psychopaths or serial killers, for example), but most horror novels go beyond a mere human to a figure with some kind of supernatural element.

CORE TITLE

★*The Monstrumologist,* by Rick Yancey (Printz Honor, BBYA, AAYA 2010; PPYA 2017)

Will Henry has been apprenticed to the monstrumologist Dr. Walthrop after the mysterious death of Will's parents. (A monstrumologist is someone who studies monsters.) Will is treated poorly and forced to assist with gruesome scientific experiments. The novel consists of Will's found journals, and their somewhat old-fashioned language places the reader in the nineteenth century and adds a necessary linguistic remove, without which the book's gory details might be too

---

Young adult books with particular appeal for adult readers are designated with a star (★).

scary for some teens. The remains of a seventeen-year-old girl are discovered, impregnated by a monster in the grave. Dr. Walthrop determines that a pod of Anthropophagi, headless beasts that feed on human flesh using the teeth in their stomach, has infested a nearby New England town. How did these creatures make their way to America, and how will Walthrop and Will destroy them? Yancey is a master at creating foreboding and simultaneously moving the plot forward. This is a plot-driven novel that incorporates an intriguing mix of science, legend, and myth. Readers experience jolts of adrenaline as the initial claustrophobic tension spills into one action scene after another. The *Monstrumologist* series raises ethical questions that grow darker as it continues.

NEXT READS

Rotters, by Daniel Kraus (Odyssey Award, AAYA 2012)

This contemporary, realistic horror novel follows sixteen-year-old Joey, who is forced to move from Chicago to small-town Iowa to live with his estranged father after his mother dies in a tragic accident. Rejected by his new classmates and left to fend for himself by a mostly absent parent, Joey reluctantly decides to follow in his father's footsteps, eschewing all normal life to become a grave robber. This novel shares elements with *The Monstrumologist,* including graveyard scenes and a vulnerable young protagonist who is under the protection of an untrustworthy guardian. But its setting is so different that they are very different books, even though they are stories that might appeal to the same reader. Joey's father's fellow gravediggers, a gruesome brotherhood, are a terrifying group, and none more than his archrival. The stakes grow surprisingly high. The *Rotters* audiobook won the 2012 Odyssey Award.

Bird Box, by Josh Malerman (PPYA 2017)

This adult novel proves that sometimes the unknown monster is the worst terror of all. First in Russia, then Alaska, and then across the United States, people begin seeing something so terrifying that they attack those around them, and then take their own lives. Malorie and her sister were living in their very first apartment, outside Detroit, when the phenomenon began. Four years later, Malorie lives with two small children in a house near the river. Every door is locked, every window is sealed. But now it's time to row down the river to find a safer situation. Blindfolded. With unseen creatures all around them.

This is psychological horror at its best, in a novel that maintains a high level of tension from page one. Malorie feels young and alone, which resonates with teens.

NOS4A2, by Joe Hill

When this adult novel opens, Vic is eight years old and riding her new bike as fast as she can across the Shorter Way Bridge. She rides that bike into another place entirely and finds something that's been lost. As a teen, blowing off steam after a fight with her mom, she rides straight through to the house of Charlie Manx, a man who drives a 1930 black Rolls-Royce Wraith, license plate NOS4A2. Manx is an indefinable monster who sucks the life-force out of the kids he abducts and then drops in Christmasland. NOS4A2 has natural appeal for teens thanks to the pacing, Vic's bravery, and the clever use of Christmas as a subject of horror. Mostly, for all his novel's darkness, Hill has a great time telling his sprawling story, and that enthusiasm is infectious.

Zombies

Zombies are terrifying because they are single-mindedly out to eat human flesh. They're heartbreaking because they used to be human, even friends or family. Zombie infestations are often part of a post-apocalyptic world, caused by a pandemic of some kind, and origin stories are part of this subgenre's appeal. Many zombie novels center around people dealing with the collapse of organized society, and enduring daily fear and hopelessness. In some YA zombie novels, groups of teens are on their own in a world overrun by zombies, creating new rules for survival.

CORE TITLE

Rot & Ruin, by Jonathan Maberry (BBYA 2011; PPYA 2016)

When Benny Imura turns fifteen, he apprentices as a bounty hunter with his older brother, Tom. They live out west, and are safe inside fences. Benny's first expedition into the Rot and Ruin, a post-apocalyptic wasteland, is terrifying. But Tom's job is not what Benny assumed. Tom is hired by the family members of zombies to find and "quiet" them in the most merciful, humane way possible. The real terrors are Charlie "Pink-Eye" Matthias and Motor City Hammer—bounty hunters who torture zombies for fun. They run Gameland, where kidnapped children are forced to fight zombies to the death. Part of this novel's appeal is the determination of Benny and his friends to improve their world. They train in the use of weapons and make themselves stronger, and then they take risks for what they believe in. This is an emotional read which inspires fear, sadness over the loss of the old world, and anger at the inhumanity of man. At the same time, this first in a series is full of action and is great for reluctant readers.

NEXT READS

This Is Not a Test, by Courtney Summers (BFYA, QP Top Ten 2013; PPYA 2017)

Sloane's older sister Lily has run away from home and left her alone with their monster of a father, who beats them, so Sloane plans to commit suicide. These plans are interrupted by a zombie apocalypse. Thirteen pages into the story, Sloane is trapped inside her suburban high school with five other teenagers, trying to keep the zombies from breaking in. Sloane tells her own story, and it is one of utter despair. She doesn't care if she lives or dies, nor understand why the others fight so hard. But she also doesn't want her actions to get anyone else killed. The group dynamics inside are almost as stressful as the zombies outside. This book is ideal for readers who like elements of realist fiction and psychological horror alongside their zombies.

★*Ashes,* by Isla J. Bick (QP 2013)

Alex refuses further treatment for a brain tumor and heads to the mountains for one last solo camping trip. While she's there, multiple EMPs (electromagnetic pulses) are released above the Earth. Most adults die instantly, and teens become the Changed, monsters who eat flesh. Alex does not change, however, and in order to survive, she joins forces with others who remain unchanged—a young girl who was out hiking with her grandfather, and a young soldier suffering from post-traumatic stress disorder. Teens who love *The Walking Dead,* whether the television or graphic novel series, will find a similar situation here. The human survivors become more of a threat than the zombies themselves. Gruesome violence places the appeal of this science fiction/horror blend firmly in the horror category. The book is the first in the *Ashes* trilogy.

The Girl with All the Gifts, by M. R. Carey

This novel bears special mention thanks to its unique twist on the post-apocalyptic zombie novel. Melanie is a young teen who might be the only hope in a world devastated twenty years earlier by a virulent fungus. She has a genius IQ and loves school, and especially her teacher, Miss Justineau. So why does Melanie spend her classroom time muzzled and locked into a wheelchair, and the remaining hours locked in a cell? Why is she being studied by a scientist? After the military compound where she lives is attacked by the walking dead, Melanie and her caretakers flee across England searching for a safe haven named Beacon. This is an unpredictable, character- and action-driven novel that goes beyond the expectations of the horror genre. The 2016 movie adaptation received raves.

Vampires

Here we are not interested in the romantic vampire. Instead, we speak of the horrifying, the murderous, the violent, of immortal creatures without souls. The undead. In general, vampires that inspire fear fare better in adult crossover titles than in YA literature itself, which is packed with sensual, romantic vampires. But there are exceptions. The vampire tradition began with Bram Stoker's nineteenth-century novel *Dracula,* and this is one classic that teens seek out of their own volition. They want to know the "original" story, and this book's mixture of letters, journals, diaries, and newspaper articles keeps the story moving.

CORE TITLE

The Coldest Girl in Coldtown, by Holly Black (BFYA, AAYA 2014; PPYA 2016)

> This gritty thriller is full of chilling moments, especially the book's opening in which Tana wakes up the morning after a party in the middle of the remains of a brutal, deadly vampire attack. The other two survivors are a madly handsome vampire and Tana's ex-boyfriend, who is infected. She escapes with them to a nearby Coldtown, a walled, ghetto-like city where vampires are imprisoned to prevent the spread of their kind, and from which their lives (and glamorous parties) are broadcast to a world obsessed with them. While some wish to be turned into vampires, Tana isn't sure she wants to give up her human existence just yet. But entering a Coldtown means she can never go back. Or does it? This is a fresh look at how vampires might figure into our world, one unique in YA fiction. And on top of the appeal of excellent world-building, horror readers will find a fully

realized heroine, a fascinating developing romantic relationship, and a sharply imagined reality TV angle.

NEXT READS

★*Peeps*, by Scott Westerfeld (BBYA, TTT 2006)

In a dark and dangerous New York City that will appeal to urban fantasy readers, Cal Thompson is infected on the night he loses his virginity. Vampirism is a sexually transmitted parasitic disease that causes people to become violently cannibalistic monsters called "peeps." But Cal's infection is different. It gives him powers without making him violent. He's no threat as long as he remains celibate. So he drops his college plans and works for the Night Watch, a city agency charged with finding and capturing peeps. Cal runs into a conspiracy on the job that hints at a long-held secret about vampirism. He also meets an appealing love interest. His story is interspersed with chapters about parasites in nature, which is enough to give readers additional shivers.

Salem's Lot, by Stephen King

The master of horror addressed the undead early in his career in this terrifying story of vampires that overrun a small New England town called Jerusalem's Lot (shortened to Salem's Lot). While there is nothing particularly "teen" about this novel—it follows a writer who returns to the town where he grew up in order to write his next novel—it is a reading experience that is impossible to put down. It begins with a long buildup, giving readers plenty of time to dread the horrors to come. It also gives them time to know and care about the townsfolk before they encounter the vampires among them. And they do encounter vampires, in a second half which takes place in the space of just two days, never slowing for a moment. This was the first of King's novels set in small-town Maine, and Jerusalem's Lot is an unforgettable setting in itself.

The Historian, by Elizabeth Kostova

It all begins when a sixteen-year-old girl discovers a book and cache of letters in her father's library, which reveals a possible family connection to Vlad the Impaler. Indeed, these documents imply that Dracula is still alive. Unfortunately, her father disappears before she can learn more, so she sets out to find him. The pleasures of this lengthy novel include an increasingly intense sense of approaching terror, the occasional sudden scare, the mystery of the girl's mother's disappearance, beautiful writing, and a satisfying climactic conclusion. The book also takes the reader around Europe, to both famous and lesser-known locations. Much of the novel unfolds in letters and flashbacks, echoing Stoker's *Dracula*. *The Historian* is a blend of different genres, with elements of mystery, thriller, and romance, and is suggested for teens who enjoy tackling a longer, literary challenge.

Gothic Horror

Gothic fiction emphasizes atmosphere and setting. It is often set in the past, in an isolated, decrepit house, castle, village, or asylum. Gothic novels are known for a foreboding atmosphere and slowly revealed secrets. The pace may be slower and, in general, this subgenre offers less gore and fewer shocks, so its titles can be recommended to readers who want to be creeped out—but not grossed out or terrified. It is also popular with readers who enjoy unreliable narrators, especially narrators who doubt their own sanity.

CORE TITLE

This Dark Endeavor: The Apprenticeship of Victor Frankenstein, by Kenneth Oppel (BFYA 2012)

The Frankensteins live in a beautiful château on a lake outside Geneva, Switzerland. Sixteen-year-old Victor and his twin, Konrad, share their home with Elizabeth, who was taken in by their father after losing her own parents. Konrad is the golden boy, the light to Victor's dark, and Victor's jealousy grows deeper when he discovers that Elizabeth and Konrad are in love. One afternoon, Victor, Konrad, and Elizabeth discover an old library in a secret passageway, a Biblioteca Obscura of forbidden books on the occult arts of healing and alchemy. Soon after, Konrad falls ill and Victor uses the forbidden library to find a cure. This is a well-written story that gradually reveals itself, with the added appeal of excellent character development and exotic locations. And there is horror and gore by the end—scary expeditions to collect ingredients for Konrad's cure, including a body part of the person closest to him. This book is notable for being a prequel to Mary Shelley's classic novel *Frankenstein*. This is the first in the *Apprenticeship of Victor Frankenstein* series.

NEXT READS

★*Long Lankin,* by Lindsey Barraclough (BFYA 2013; PPYA 2017)

In 1958, two sisters are dropped off outside a small English village and are left to find the path to Guerdon Hall, their Aunt Ida's house. Their aunt is *not* happy to see them. The house is full of cobwebs hanging down in loops, thick dust, scary portraits, ivy growing inside the house, hidden rooms, deep scratches in each door, a ghost, and no telephone or other connection to the outside world. The house sits among tidal pools between the river and the sea, "half sinking into the ground." A horror that has stalked the village children for centuries returns when the sisters begin to investigate the old churchyard. Dense prose and alternating first-person narratives make this book perfect for strong readers who love to soak up the details leading to the horror. This book delivers real terrors in the end. It is the first in a duology.

And the Trees Crept In, by Dawn Kurtagich

The plot of this book sounds similar to *Long Lankin,* but Kurtagich creates a very different reading experience. Two sisters run away from abusive parents in London to their aunt's blood-red house in the middle of the woods. Their aunt has a mental breakdown and retreats to the attic after warning them never to enter the woods. But there's no other way to reach civilization, where food and luxuries like the Internet still exist. Unless World War III has begun. The garden dies as the forest edges closer and closer to the house, and the younger sister hides her playtime with the Creeper Man. The writing is spare, encompassing flashbacks, multiple versions of events, and each sister's notes to herself. The overwhelming feeling is one of disorientation in this psychological horror novel with all the trappings of the gothic.

★*Miss Peregrine's Home for Peculiar Children,* by Ransom Riggs (BFYA, TTT 2012)

Sixteen-year-old Jacob travels to an island off the coast of Wales to explore the abandoned orphanage where his grandfather was sheltered during World War II. The unusual children that his grandfather told Jacob about are still there, and in danger. This book is just scary enough to qualify as horror, though mostly it is mysterious and creepy, as Jacob uncovers both secrets and monsters. The cover of this unique book is a teen magnet, as are the haunting period photographs interspersed throughout. Fans of found footage movies may find a similar appeal here. This is the first in a popular series, which spawned graphic novel versions illustrated by Jean Cassandra, who has been praised for effectively incorporating the original book's photographs. A movie adaptation was released in 2016.

Ghost Stories and the Occult

Ghost stories are the bedrock of the horror genre. By the teen years, ghost stories have expanded beyond the haunted house into tales of possession, witches and demons, and malevolent spirits and curses. Often the appeal includes solving the mystery of why the spirits of the dead are lingering. What do they want? What causes them to possess or haunt? Why aren't they at peace, or what are they protecting? Teens also enjoy the courage of the characters who are brave enough to stand up to them. But then again, sometimes the teens *are* the possessed.

CORE TITLE

Anna Dressed in Blood, by Kendare Blake (BFYA, QP 2012; PPYA 2017)

Three years ago, seventeen-year-old Cas Lowood took over his father's job of dispatching violent ghosts and inherited both his father's talent and his knife. His current job takes Cas and his mother to Thunder Bay, Ontario, where he meets his match in the ghost of Anna Korlov, known as Anna Dressed in Blood. This briskly paced novel is wonderfully atmospheric, from the beaches and cliffs of Thunder Bay to the old haunted house that Anna inhabits. Cas makes new friends at school, and each of them is a wonderfully developed character— including a good male friend who helps him confront Anna. These teens actually talk like teens, joking through their fear. There is scary violence and frightening twists and turns to the story, especially surrounding the side plot of Cas's father's death. When his father's killer comes for him, he is more powerful than any entity Cas has challenged before. And finally, this is a horror story *and* a love story that might work for readers who enjoy paranormal literature. The book is the first in a duology.

NEXT READS

Bliss, by Lauren Myracle

It's the summer of 1969, and Bliss is left with her grandmother after her parents move to Canada. She finds herself attending the elite Crestview Academy, where she is startled by the bullying and racism she observes. But even more strange is the voice that only she can hear, calling to her from a locked upper floor of the main classroom building, "*You are the real key, you are flesh and blood.*" Bliss befriends a bullied outcast, only to realize that she has attached herself to a girl who is determined to bring a malevolent spirit back from the dead. Myracle ratchets up the tension by incorporating the misuse of holy relics, creepy anonymous journal entries, and newspaper headlines about the Charles Manson murders. This book also features the most awkward and horrifying sleepover *ever.*

★*The Diviners,* by Libba Bray (BFYA Top Ten, AAYA 2013; PPYA 2017)

This sprawling first book in a series brings 1920s Prohibition-era New York City to witty life, while mixing in a serial killer, an ancient evil, and several young people with unusual abilities. It all begins with Evie, newly arrived from Ohio to visit her uncle who runs the Museum of American Folklore, Superstition, and the Occult. Evie's winningly sharp sense of humor and her enthusiasm for all things flapper bring the fun, while her ability to learn about a person by touching anything they own kicks off the foreboding. This novel could easily be listed under historical fiction, suspense, or fantasy. It landed here because its paranormal killer, Naughty John, is one scary dude, and the story turns into a big battle between good and (supernatural) evil. The audiobook of *The Diviners* is also highly recommended.

Locke & Key, by Joe Hill, illustrated by Gabriel Rodriguez (GGNT 2010; PPYA 2017)

This six-volume adult graphic novel series features the Locke family, with sons Tyler, Kinsey, and Bode and their mother. They move into Keyhouse, a mansion in Lovecraft, Massachusetts, after their father is murdered by two teenagers. Right away the boys start finding secrets in the house, including a door that separates the spirit from the body, a ghost in the well, and demons locked away in keys. Their discoveries become progressively more dangerous, with possession and murder the result. The story's origins go all the way back to the Revolutionary War, and the climax takes place at a modern-day after-prom party. In other words, although high school is only one of the settings and only a couple of the characters are teens, this is an ideal crossover series for teen horror readers.

Expanding Readers' Horizons into the Whole Collection

Movies

Teens are well-known lovers of horror movies, as Hollywood marketers well know.

Movies—Series

The Evil Dead

Friends in a remote cabin encounter demons. Also *Evil Dead II and* 2015's *Ash vs Evil Dead.*

I Know What You Did Last Summer

Four teenagers cover up a hit-and-run accident. Then someone begins taking revenge. Adapted from the novel by Lois Duncan.

Paranormal Activity

Strange happenings in a suburban home prompt the owners to set up camcorders and learn that the house is possessed. Five sequels and counting.

Scream

A masked killer picks off teenagers one by one in a small town.

Movies—Stand-Alones

Blair Witch Project

College students go into the woods to make a movie about the Blair Witch legend. Only their footage is recovered. Also the more recent *Blair Witch.*

The Cabin in the Woods

College students drive to a cabin in the woods, where they are picked off one by one.

The Exorcist

> The demonic possession of a young girl and the Catholic priest determined to save her.

House at the End of the Street

> A teen and her mother move to a new town, and end up living next to a house where a girl murdered her parents. The teen befriends the killer's brother.

It

> A faithful adaptation of the novel by Stephen King. *It: Chapter Two* is scheduled for 2019.

Television

Buffy the Vampire Slayer

> Written and directed by Joss Whedon. Seven seasons of the TV show were followed up by graphic novels written by Joss Whedon himself, referred to as Seasons 8, 9, and 10.

The Exorcist

> Based on the horror classic.

Scream

> Based on the movie franchise.

Stranger Things

> SF/horror/mystery thriller.

Supernatural

> Demon-hunting brothers on the CW Television Network.

The Walking Dead

> Zombie thriller inspired by the Eisner Award-winning graphic novel series of the same name by Robert Kirkman and Tony Moore.

Recommendations for Readers' Advisory

Horror is a tough genre for librarians who do not read it themselves. There are fewer horror novels that cross over into literary fiction, mystery, historical fiction, or other popular genres to help give non-horror readers some scaffolding.

Also, patrons who love watching horror movies or television may not have any interest in reading horror, and vice versa. Viewing and reading are very different things when it comes to horror. Watching a movie leaves little to the imagination. Reading a book allows the reader to determine the imagery. Sometimes this can be even scarier, but it also means that the mind can refuse to go certain places, whereas it has no choice at the movies. It is impossible to "un-see" the images on a screen. Still, if a reader comes looking for recommendations, it is not a bad strategy to use movies as a common ground for determining their interests and tolerance levels.

This is a genre in which crossover suggestions must be considered carefully. Adult horror can mix sex, violence, and even torture in ways that are too disturbing for teen readers. Most authors writing for the teen audience stay within certain bounds. But it is important to read reviews carefully, and consult the resources given below.

Keeping Up with New and Upcoming Titles

Journals

Booklist's annual August Spotlight on SF/Fantasy & Horror issue includes Top 10 lists, special articles, and interviews. I also recommend keeping an eye on book reviews by Becky Spratford and Daniel Kraus.

VOYA (Voice of Youth Advocates) Magazine includes an annual Best Science Fiction, Fantasy, Horror list in the April issue.

Websites

Common Sense Media: www.commonsensemedia.org/movie-lists/best-horror-movies
Information on horror movies, including levels of violence and sexuality.

Horror Writers Association: http://horror.org/hwa-reading-list/
The association compiles an annual Reading List.

RA for All: Horror: http://raforallhorror.blogspot.com/
The online home for the *Readers' Advisory Guide to Horror*, maintained by its author, Rebecca Siegel Spratford (Becky Spratford). This is mainly for adult readers and librarians, but teen appeal is mentioned on occasion. Bonus: each October features 31 Days of Horror.

Something Wicked This Way Comes: http://somethingwicked
comesofage.tumblr.com/

> This tumblr by librarians Paula Gallagher and Paula Willey keeps up
> with the latest in horror with teen appeal.

Stephen King Rereads

For young people coming to Stephen King for the first time, and for librarians interested in knowing more about each Stephen King title without reading (or rereading) every single one, these sites are intelligent, entertaining, and informative.

Booklist

> www.booklistreader.com/2017/06/28/books-and-authors/stephen
> -kings-it-parade-week-1-is-that-a-book-or-a-bible/

The Guardian

> www.theguardian.com/books/series/rereading-stephen-king

Tor

> www.tor.com/features/series/the-great-stephen-king-reread

Awards and Lists

Aurealis Awards (for Australian speculative fiction): https://
aurealisawards.org/

Bram Stoker Awards, which include a Young Adult novel category www
.horror.org/awards/stokers.htm

> This is the only award that includes a specific category for YA horror.

The RUSA Reading List includes a horror category: www.ala.org/rusa/
awards/readinglist

> This is for adult fiction, which does sometimes cross over.

Shirley Jackson Awards: www.shirleyjacksonawards.org/

Print Resources

Jensen, Kelly. "Horror in YA Lit Is a Staple, Not a Trend." *School
Library Journal*. September 2013. www.slj.com/2013/09/collection
-development/horror-in-ya-lit-is-a-staple-not-a-trend/#_.

Orr, Cynthia, and Diana Tixier Herald, eds. *Genreflecting: A Guide to Popular Reading Interests*. Santa Barbara, CA: Libraries Unlimited, 2013.

Saricks, Joyce. *The Readers' Advisory Guide to Genre Fiction*. 2nd ed. Chicago: American Library Association, 2009.

Spratford, Becky Siegel. *The Readers' Advisory Guide to Horror*. 2nd ed. Chicago: American Library Association, 2012.

NOTES

1. Joyce G. Saricks, *The Readers' Advisory Guide to Genre Fiction*, 2nd ed. (Chicago: American Library Association, 2009), 112; Becky Siegel Spratford, *The Readers' Advisory Guide to Horror*, 2nd ed. (Chicago: American Library Association, 2012), 13–14.

2. Saricks makes this point about the horror genre in general on p. 114 of *The Readers' Advisory Guide to Genre Fiction*. I found this to be true as I studied the YA examples of the genre.

3. Saricks, *The Readers' Advisory Guide to Genre Fiction*, 121 and 123.

4. Stephanie L. Maatta, *A Few Good Books: Using Contemporary Readers' Advisory Strategies to Connect Readers with Books* (New York: Neal-Schuman, 2010), 163.

5. Ibid.

10

Historical Fiction

Carrie Shaurette

I n this chapter, historical fiction is defined as a narrative centered around an actual past time, place, or event. While some of the characters may be based on real people, the author takes liberties in creating fictional individuals to move along the plot. This is often explained in an author's note at the end of the book, which should help readers distinguish facts from fiction.

Though historical fiction is often a beloved genre for adults, it can experience an image problem among teens. As Jennifer Hubert states, many teens have a prejudice against historical fiction since it has gone through the death knell of being assigned in class, so their perceptions can work against it. "It also might be because they're not reading the right kinds of historical fiction. You know the kind I mean—the kind that's full of pirates, prostitutes, witches, jewel thieves, wise men, fools, kings, queens, patriots, and survivors."[1] Humorous books like *My Lady Jane* by Cynthia Hand, Brodi Ashton, and Jodi Meadows will work for any teen who appreciates tongue-in-cheek wit and political intrigue.

Storylines may vary greatly within the genre, but teens will always want to read about themes with which they can connect. Despite the 1920s

Since receiving her MSLIS from Pratt Institute in 2010, **Carrie Shaurette** has been a librarian working with middle and high school students at Dwight-Englewood School for the past eight years. She reviews books for *School Library Journal* and Adult Books 4 Teens column and served as a member of the 2018 YALSA Best Books for Young Adults committee.

setting in *The Steep and Thorny Way,* today's teens will identify with the homophobia and racial prejudice that Joe and Hanalee must face. A truly engrossing novel will tackle issues faced throughout history such as discrimination, war, natural resources, religion, and power, and it will make them relevant to our current day.

Standouts in the genre build a strong sense of place and time, with precise re-creations of historical environments. While some authors write sporadically in this genre, others have become recognizable names for solid historical fiction, each writing in his or her own distinct style. Teens who like a mashup of genres will appreciate Libba Bray and particularly her *Diviners* series, which blends magic and horror in the 1920s. Walter Dean Myers, Stacey Lee, and Joseph Bruchac all focus on diverse voices throughout history, and teens who enjoy Myers's realistic fiction will find that his accessible writing style and emphasis on social justice issues carry over to historical fiction like *Riot* and *Invasion* as well. Michael Morpurgo's *Private Peaceful* and Elizabeth Wein's *Young Pilots* series will appeal to teens wanting to read about the grittier side of war. Laurie Halse Anderson's legion of realistic fiction fans may cross genres to read her trilogy for younger teens, *Seeds of America,* which is set during the Revolutionary War.

Because of its connection to history, this category shares traits with nonfiction narratives and historical memoirs, but while sticking to the facts is crucial in nonfiction, historical fiction can embellish the truth to serve the story. However, some readers will happily cross over into both genres, enjoying the balance between the entertainment of historical fiction and the education of nonfiction. With a popular time period such as World War II, teens who responded positively to historical fiction like *The Book Thief* by Marcus Zusak or *Anna and the Swallow Man* by Gavriel Savit may be interested in reading a memoir like Elie Wiesel's *Night,* or a graphic novel like Art Spiegelman's *Maus.*

Appeal

While many elements of historical fiction can appeal to teens, the way it is presented to them is potentially the most important aspect of whether they will pick it up. While historical fiction isn't always the best starting place for reluctant readers, and the genre's appeal for teens has long been underrated, there are plenty of esteemed titles and perennial favorites, particularly for avid book lovers.

Setting

Since the setting is crucial in historical fiction, the way it is depicted can make or break a title. Inaccuracy or insufficiency of detail can detract from any story set in the past. Some teens become invested in a particular era of history, such as World War II, with novels like Ruta Sepetys's *Salt to the Sea* and *Between Shades of Gray*. If teens want to dive into ancient cultures like Greece, Egypt, or Rome, they may enjoy books from Michelle Moran's *Ancient Egypt* series such as *Cleopatra's Daughter*, or the Trojan War novel *The Song of Achilles* by Madeline Miller. Other teens will enjoy the romance and court drama of Jane Yolen's *The Queen's Own Fool: A Novel of Mary Queen of Scots*, or Tudor-era novels like Philippa Gregory's *The Other Boleyn Girl*.

Pacing

While certain subgenres like war or historical thrillers will provide more action that quickens the pace, books set in the past tend to be more leisurely paced because of the wealth of detail that is required to establish their setting. For example, the danger involved in being a World War II pilot quickens the pace in *Flygirl* by Sherri Smith, though some necessary context about prejudice against a black female filling this role in 1941 unavoidably slows down the reading experience. Since the historical context must be introduced early on, according to Joyce Saricks, "there is an immediacy to the pacing that pulls the reader quickly into the story."[2]

Tone

Depending on the subgenre of historical fiction, tone could range from formal and serious in a more traditional title to impassioned and angry in a book dealing with social justice. As an example of the wide variety often found, consider the difference of tone between two titles that fall under the war subgenre and deal with dark subjects: *Fallen Angels* is grim and bleak, while *Code Name Verity* is frenzied and impassioned.

Characterization

The characters in this genre are often a mixture of actual historical figures and fictional individuals who help move the story along. While the protagonists are typically teenagers, there is frequently a large cast of individuals of all ages which helps provide historical context, and they are sometimes included in a genealogy chart or character introduction at the beginning. It is important for the characters to follow the social culture of their respective time periods. Terms and phrases from modern times and other anachronisms should be avoided. In spite of living in quite different circumstances from the historical characters, teens should be able to relate to these characters and their motivations and decisions. While most teens have not seen active combat, they will understand the way Ana feels the need to hide a part of her past from those around her in *Girl at War*.

Story/Theme

While setting and characters are very important in historical fiction, the leisurely pace necessitates an engaging story to entice the reader to continue reading. Even within a historical context, teens should be able to connect with the issues and conflicts presented in the book. In a particularly successful example, teens interested in human rights easily empathize with Arn's plight during the Cambodian genocide as he is forced into becoming a Khmer Rouge child soldier in *Never Fall Down* by Patricia McCormick.

Key Subgenres and Core Titles in Historical Fiction

The five subgenres explored here are meant to give a broad overview instead of a deep dive into any one historical event or time period, and thus reflect the varied mixtures or mashups that are often explored in books written for young adults.

Classic and Traditional

Teens who enjoy luxuriating in a different time and place will flock to traditional historical fiction. With its attention to historical detail and focus on complex characters, this subgenre is more leisurely paced and often features female protagonists. Since the traditional label applies more to story than format, books like the 1920s coming-of-age tale *The Scrapbook of Frankie Pratt* which features memorabilia such as letters, advertisements, and other appropriate period items can also fall into this category.

Readers who enjoy nineteenth-century novels like *Little Women, Jane Eyre,* or the works of Jane Austen will recognize and welcome the similarities of characters and themes they find between these classic works and today's historical novels.

CORE TITLE

★*Between Shades of Gray,* by Ruta Sepetys (BFYA, Morris Finalist 2012; PPYA 2014; Golden Kite Award)

> After the Soviet secret police barge into her home one night in 1941, fifteen-year-old Lina, her mother, and her younger brother are taken to a work camp in Siberia, and they are separated from her father, who has been sentenced to death. To survive in a place with brutal soldiers, rampant starvation, and freezing temperatures, many characters must make difficult choices, including lying, betrayal, and prostitution. However, even in dark times, hope is found in Lina's romantic relationship with Andrius. Whether or not they are artists themselves, teens will appreciate the way Lina uses her drawings to get herself through this difficult time. During flashbacks, readers get to know of Lina's previous life in Lithuania, which forms a stark contrast with her current situation. Teens and adults, for whom this is a potential crossover title, who enjoy reading World War II literature may be drawn to the new and unfamiliar setting of the Soviet oppression of people from the Baltic states. This book would work for teens wanting to read about the darker side of history and humanity.

NEXT READS

The Hired Girl, by Laura Amy Schlitz (BFYA, Horn Book Honor 2016; O'Dell, Sydney Taylor, National Jewish Book Award)

> After being mistreated by her father and brothers on the family farm, fourteen-year-old Joan Skraggs runs away in search of employment and true love. In the summer of 1911, the only job that Joan can find is as a hired girl for a Jewish family, which conflicts with her own Catholic upbringing. It is during this job that Joan experiences her first crush while learning to cook and clean for a family that is very different from her own. Because the book is told through a diary format, readers can get inside Joan's mind, and while they won't always

---

Young adult books with particular appeal for adult readers are designated with a star (★).

agree with her impulsive decisions, they will root for her success. Her improper infatuation with an older boy, along with the diary format, will pull in younger teens. This traditional coming-of-age novel reads like a modern classic and will appeal to readers of books like *Anne of Green Gables* or *Pollyanna*.

A Northern Light, by Jennifer Donnelly (BBYA, Printz Honor 2004; PPYA 2011)

When the dead body of a young woman washes ashore in the Adirondack Mountains in the summer of 1906, the sixteen-year-old precocious wordsmith Mattie Gokey is working at a hotel and trying to decide whether to study writing at Barnard College in New York City or to stay home near her family, get married, and begin a traditional farm wife's existence. The mystery of the dead woman and her missing boyfriend is based on actual events, though it's more a slow reveal than a clue-filled tale of suspense. This is a good choice for readers who like a plethora of detail. With Mattie's vocabulary word of the day sprinkled throughout, this book will appeal to young writers and feminists. In fact, what shines in addition to Mattie's budding romance is the exploration of the limited choices available for young women in the early twentieth century. This book was recognized by the Amelia Bloomer list of the best feminist books for young readers.

The Snow in August, by Pete Hamill (Alex 1998)

After eleven-year-old Michael Devlin witnesses a bigoted act of violence in his 1940s working-class Brooklyn neighborhood, he wrestles with his personal set of ethics. Michael is a Catholic altar boy, and his world opens when he befriends a rabbi from Prague and begins learning about Jewish history and folklore. When Michael is accused of snitching on the local thug who committed the violent crime, Rabbi Hirsch guides Michael on his path to honorable retaliation, which leads to a showdown with a mythical creature. As Rabbi Hirsch states, if "you keep quiet about some crimes, it's just as bad as the crime." Teens with an interest in Marvel comics will appreciate the parallels with Captain America, while baseball fans will latch on to the Jackie Robinson storyline. A novel about finding courage within a difficult world, this is a perfect choice for thoughtful teens trying to figure out what kind of person they want to be.

War

Teens who enjoy reading action books may be attracted to the reality of war novels which are often based on historical events. Stories of espionage, secret codes, battlefield tactics, and the bonding that occurs among soldiers are often staples of this intense subgenre. Because realistic violence is a fundamental characteristic of war, readers must be comfortable reading scenes of carnage and bloodshed. Some teens interested in the state of armed conflicts around the world today will be pulled in by the cause and effect of historical wars, or they may have an interest in reading about military strategy and tactics.

CORE TITLE

★*Code Name Verity,* by Elizabeth Wein (BFYA Top Ten, AAYA, TTT, Printz Honor 2013; Edgar Award, Horn Book Honor 2012; PPYA 2014)

> After surviving a plane crash and subsequently sitting in a Nazi-run French jail cell, detained prisoner Julie (aka Queenie, Verity, Eva, or Katharina) agrees to unveil secrets about the British war effort in order to buy time and avoid further torture at the hands of her brutal captors. While she narrates with a wandering confession about the past, readers are encouraged to question her reliability with the truth as the tension builds, but what shines through is the strength of her friendship with Maddie, a pilot who would not normally run in Julie's aristocratic social circles. The more reserved Maddie narrates the book's second section, opening up a new perspective and turning Julie's narration on its head. Readers who enjoy a good twist and those who are not bothered by severe suffering will race to the finish and may wish to immediately begin again. Strong readers will appreciate the book's rich thematic content and abundant literary allusions. This World War II spy thriller, which follows the fierce friendship of two brave young women, could easily be a crossover adult title.

NEXT READS

Fallen Angels, by Walter Dean Myers

> After high school, seventeen-year-old Richie Perry enlists in the army and gets sent to fight in Vietnam. He faces drastic differences in the rank and power of commanding officers, and he must deal with racial prejudice that puts him, as a soldier of color, in added danger. Margaret A. Edwards Award winner Myers captures the anxiety and

apprehension felt by young adults sent to war and never glosses over the violence that soldiers experience as they suffer from land mines, shrapnel, and death. During his thoughtful first-person narration, Perry contemplates the morality of war while developing close relationships due to intense shared experiences. Teenagers will see parallels between the Vietnam War and current-day conflicts in the Middle East. Moreover, as a coming-of-age story set inside a war novel, this book will appeal to both readers who want to learn about the reality of combat and those interested in historical racism in the military.

Code Talker: A Novel about the Navajo Marines of World War Two, by Joseph Bruchac (BBYA 2006, PPYA 2014)

After the Japanese attack Pearl Harbor in 1941, sixteen-year-old Ned Begay is eager to join the fight, and so he enlists in the Marine Corps despite his young age. As a young Navajo, his ethnicity was often denigrated by white men who wanted to eliminate the culture of all Indians, but his tribe's obscure language puts Ned and other Navajos in a unique position to provide a hidden code for American soldiers in combat. Because grown-up Ned tells his story in accessible language to his grandchildren who have asked about his medal, the reader feels immediately connected with him and is pulled directly into the narrative. Fans of action will appreciate the vivid fighting at battles like Iwo Jima and will eagerly admire the proven bravery of World War II soldiers, while teens interested in secret codes or Native American history will also connect to this war novel.

Girl at War, by Sara Novic (Alex 2016)

During the Yugoslavian civil war of the 1990s, Ana's parents are brutally murdered in front of her. She ends up fighting as a child soldier before managing an escape to the United States to be with her baby sister, where they are raised by an adoptive family. The narrative jumps back and forth between the ten-year-old girl caught in the civil war and the twenty-year-old who hasn't attempted to deal with all the horror she experienced. With a combination of war scenes interwoven with boyfriend and family struggles, readers will feel the conflict between Ana's two worlds as she wrestles with her identity. This book will appeal to anyone who has ever felt isolated because of their culture, as well as those looking to learn more about a brutal conflict that is not often written about for young adults.

Injustice throughout History

Historical fiction can be a way to look back at time periods when one group of people behaved unjustly to another because of racial prejudice and discrimination. Series like Laurie Halse Anderson's *Seeds of America*, beginning with *Chains*, or Mildred D. Taylor's *Logan Family* series, starting with *Roll of Thunder, Hear My Cry*, explore racial injustice in American history. The books listed below use fictional characters to address weighty issues of inequality throughout history. This section will attract fairminded teens with an interest in social justice who are eager to make a difference in the world.

CORE TITLE

Day of Tears: A Novel in Dialogue, by Julian Lester (BBYA 2006)

Pierce M. Butler was a real-life figure who sold half the slaves from his plantation on one rainy, dreary day in 1859 in order to settle his gambling debts. In this setting of the largest slave auction ever held in the United States, readers come to hear about the horrendous day through the accounts of over twenty affected people from families that were separated. Teens will connect with Emma, who, twelve years old at the start of the novel and in charge of raising Butler's daughters, gets torn from her family without even the chance to say goodbye. The "dialogue" referenced in the subtitle allows for the speech and personal thoughts of each character to shine through. This, coupled with interludes where various characters look back upon the awful day of the slave auction, makes for a fast-paced and emotionally intense read. This would be an ideal book for a younger teen, and older teens looking to read a story about the horrors of slavery will also find it of interest despite the main character's young age at the beginning of the novel.

NEXT READS

The Steep and Thorny Way, by Cat Winters (BFYA 2017)

Joe Adder went to prison for running over Hanalee's African American father with his car, though he claims to be innocent of the murder. Set against a backdrop of Prohibition, the mystery of the father's death unravels through a web of bootleggers, Ku Klux Klan members, and eugenics advocates in small-town Oregon during the 1920s. The woodsy setting is vividly portrayed, and the interspersing of historical photographs within the text adds some visual atmosphere. Teens familiar with *Hamlet* will recognize parallels with that play's plot, though the focus remains more on issues of social justice as Hanalee struggles to find her place in a town that isn't ready for a strong, smart biracial young woman to thrive. With a lot packed in, including a clandestine gay relationship, this title is recommended for readers who are looking for a compelling mystery set within a bigoted historical town.

★*Out of Darkness,* by Ashley Hope Perez (Américas, BFYA, Printz Honor 2016)

After coming to live with an abusive stepfather in a small Texas town, Naomi faces severe racism, which escalates after a deadly 1937 school explosion causes local tensions to rise. When she moves there from San Antonio, Naomi brings her half-brother and half-sister, whom she has been responsible for since their mother died during childbirth. While they have an easier time "passing" because of their lighter skin, Naomi is immediately ridiculed at school and discriminated against because of her background as a Mexican American. She finds solace in a romantic relationship with Wash, though because he is African American, the match is scorned by the town and their passion faces a dark and devastating turn of events. This gut-wrenching historical novel doesn't shy away from brutality and delves deeply into issues of prejudice. Older teens and adults will painfully ache for the racially diverse, star-crossed lovers.

Mudbound, by Hillary Jordan (Alex 2009; PPYA 2014; PEN/ Bellwether Prize)

Two families collide over racial prejudice in a small Mississippi town after World War II. Because he is the father of her beloved husband Henry, Laura must abide her father-in-law Pappy's brash chauvinism and prejudice. Despite the local friction, Laura and her brother-in-law Jamie befriend a neighboring family of black sharecroppers, though when disagreements flare, the tension rises until it bursts in a dramatic climax. Teens who enjoy reading a story from multiple perspectives will appreciate that six different narrators tell the story from their own angle. This book was a winner of the Bellwether Prize for socially engaged fiction and was made into a critically acclaimed film. The novel, which focuses on the importance of diverse friendships and the courage of standing up to family, will appeal to thoughtful teens who are seeking to reflect upon and learn from racial conflicts of the past. It would be an excellent choice for a book discussion.

Mysteries and Thrillers

Tension and excitement drive these stories because of the reader's curiosity about how they will end. Sometimes the climax is foreseeable because of historical knowledge, while often readers are given clues which lead to a big revelation near the conclusion. Generally, a more rapid pace propels this group, as in the *Finishing School* series by Gail Carriger, which opens with *Etiquette and Espionage,* where young ladies learn how to spy and kill in polite Victorian society. Often featuring exciting twists and turns, this category is likely to have the most crossover with readers who normally enjoy more action and suspense titles.

CORE TITLE

Death Cloud, by Andrew Lane (PPYA 2015)

> This series starter unveils the origins of one of the shrewdest detectives of all times, Sherlock Holmes, during his teenage years. It's the summer of 1868, and fourteen-year-old Holmes has been sent to live with distant and strange relatives in the English countryside. When he and his orphaned friend Matty stumble upon a dead body surrounded by a shadowy cloud, Holmes scoffs at the commonly accepted notion that the victims have died from the plague, and he becomes determined to find out the true cause of death. Holmes's investigations end up endangering him as he is chased and kidnapped, leading to several action-packed sequences. Of course, using his trademark wit and logic, he manages to thwart a dastardly villain at the end of this fast-paced mystery, which has been officially sanctioned by the estate of Arthur Conan Doyle. With a satisfying twist ending, this book will appeal to younger teens who appreciate piecing clues together and who want to read a mystery that is filled with adventure. Despite its lack of paranormal monsters, the mystery is similar in tone to the historical fantasy series *Jackaby.*

NEXT READS

The Watch That Ends the Night: Voices from the Titanic, by Allan Wolf (BFYA 2012, AAYA Top Ten 2013)

> As the biggest and most extravagant ship of its time, the *Titanic* was slated to carry over 2,000 souls across the Atlantic Ocean, but disaster struck when it collided with an iceberg mid-journey. This story is narrated by an eclectic cast of characters ranging from the expected (socialite Margaret Brown) to the more obscure (tailor Louis Hoffman),

and even the bizarre (a lowly ship rat). Telegraph messages, snippets of Morse code, and reports from the undertaker add an authentic feel to the tale, and teens who want to read factual biographies of the characters will find them among the thirty pages of back matter. While no one will be surprised at the outcome, readers will connect emotionally to each character as they feel the danger of the sinking ship. Written in fast-moving verse, this book will attract both readers who appreciate poetic language and those fascinated by the famous maritime disaster.

Burn Baby Burn, by Meg Medina (BFYA Top Ten 2017)

Disco music pumps through New York City in 1977 as city residents live in fear of the serial killer known as Son of Sam. Seventeen-year-old Nora is dealing with a lot of outside pressure from her unruly brother, her broke mother, and teachers who keep encouraging her to go to college, but with graduation approaching, Nora is more concerned with dancing at the disco and meeting up with the cute new guy at work. She does feel the contagious terror associated with each new murder in her neighborhood, though. As fear oozes off the page in her first-person narration, it provides the perfect unnerving backdrop to complement her troubling family situation. While exciting enough for readers of true crime with a strong sense of mood, this book is essentially a portrait of a young girl finding her place in a scary world.

The Magician's Lie, by Greer Macallister

Part of the Amazing Arden's act as an illusionist is to saw a man in half, but because she grabs an ax instead of her trademark saw during her signature act one night in Iowa, she immediately becomes the prime suspect when later that evening her husband is found dead beneath a trap door in the stage. A young police officer named Virgil Holt is sent to interrogate Arden, though she claims to be innocent. The two go back and forth throughout the night as Arden divulges her dark and affecting life story up to the evening of the murder on July 23, 1905, in the hope that Holt will let her go. Teens will read with interest as they try and decide whether Arden is guilty in this briskly moving, twisty adventure. This book may appeal to readers of other adult historical novels like *Water for Elephants* or *The Night Circus*.

Literary

Strong readers who appreciate levels of meaning, depth of theme, and rich language will be drawn to literary works of historical fiction. These books move along at a more leisurely pace, using moments in history as a backdrop to tell a rich, layered story that utilizes literary elements such as metaphor, symbolism, imagery, simile, and allusion. The Printz Award, given for titles with significant literary merit, is an excellent collection development tool for books with distinguished writing, and it will lead teens to books like those in M. T. Anderson's *Astonishing Life of Octavian Nothing, Traitor to the Nation* series.

CORE TITLE

All the Light We Cannot See, by Anthony Doerr (Alex 2015, Pulitzer Prize)
Two worlds collide during World War II in the French city of Saint-Malo. Marie-Laure LeBlanc is a blind girl who finds herself, along with her uncle, involved in the French Resistance movement after her father, a locksmith for the Paris Museum of Natural History who has been entrusted with a valuable stone, is arrested. Werner Pfenning is an orphan with a knack for fixing things, especially radios. As a sixteen-year-old boy, he is drafted into the Germany military. Each character must find the courage to face a new challenge, whether it be walking down a street without sight, broadcasting secret information pulled from slips of paper that have been baked into bread loaves, or standing up against a bigger bully. With a large cast and a story that jumps through time, moving around before, during, and after the war, the narrative works like a puzzle that gradually falls into place. This is a complex coming-of-age tale written in lush poetic language that will appeal to fans of interwoven stories and World War II novels.

NEXT READS

The Lie Tree, by Frances Hardinge (BFYA Top Ten 2017, Horn Book Award 2016)
Religion and science clash as a Reverend fabricates and then shares natural scientific discoveries that are not easily explained. The center-piece of this supernatural mystery involves a tree that shares secrets with any person who whispers lies into its leaves and then spreads them around town. Faith is sure that this lie tree is involved in the death of her father, the Reverend, but she hasn't quite figured out why or how. The mood slowly builds as more information about the tree and Faith's father are revealed until the plot peaks with a tense show-down. The role of women during the Victorian era is explored in this book, which was recognized by the Amelia Bloomer feminist list. Teen readers interested in the ways for creating and preserving a female

reputation in polite society throughout history will be particularly drawn to this title.

★*The Book Thief,* by Marcus Zusak (BBYA, Printz Honor 2007; PPYA 2015, Sydney Taylor, National Jewish Book Award)

Through the haunting narration of a remorseful Grim Reaper with a daunting yet inevitable job to do, *The Book Thief* follows Liesel Meminger, a spunky orphan growing up in Nazi Germany during World War II. Liesel gets placed in foster care with the outwardly affectionate Hans and tough-as-nails Rosa. When Liesel first steals a book, she can't comprehend it because of her low reading level, but with help from Hans, she slowly learns to read. Other characters collide with Liesel as she makes friends with a neighbor boy who must join the Hitler Youth, a Jewish refugee secretly hiding in her basement, and the mayor's wife who allows Liesel to come in and read from her library. Full of symbolism and lyrical language, this complex story moves at a more measured pace and is perfect for the reader, teen or adult, who is looking for an immersive, heart-breaking experience.

★*The Passion of Dolssa,* by Julie Berry (BFYA Top Ten, Printz Honor 2017)

When a young woman accused of being a heretic and pursued by a determined friar shows up in the small town of Provensa (current-day Provence, France), she is taken in by three sisters who protect her at great personal peril. Dolssa, the young woman being chased, is a preacher with special gifts. As the leader of the sisters, Botille is a feisty matchmaker who is fluent in the social interactions of her community. This book is told through inquisitions, confessions, and testimony, and the reader experiences several distinct points of view from many different characters. While this book can be enjoyed on the surface as a suspenseful thriller, it will be cherished by teens or adults who are looking for challenging vocabulary based upon a language from the Middle Ages, and who will appreciate its layers of symbolism and meaning, and the thirty pages of back matter.

Expanding Readers' Horizons into the Whole Collection

Movies and television shows can help determine what type of historical fiction teens are interested in. Is there a particular time period they enjoy? Would they rather watch a romance or a battle?

Movies

Atonement

Thirteen-year-old Briony falsely accuses a young man of sexual assault, sending him to prison and then World War II. Based on the novel by Ian McEwan.

The Book Thief

World War II story based on the novel by Marcus Zusak.

Brooklyn

A young Irish immigrant comes to New York City in the 1950s, and she falls in love. Based on the novel by Colm Toibin.

An Education

An older man seduces sixteen-year-old Jenny Mellor in 1960s suburban London. Based on the memoir by Lynn Barber.

Forrest Gump

This upbeat movie follows a man with a low IQ through many notable moments in history from the 1960s and '70s, including the Vietnam War and Watergate. Based on the novel by Winston Groom.

The Great Gatsby

This 2013 Baz Luhrmann screen adaptation reignited interest in F. Scott Fitzgerald's classic novel of excess and doomed romance in the 1920s.

The Help

A civil rights movie highlighting the stories of African American maids. Based on the book by Kathryn Stockett.

Marie Antoinette

Tells the story of the extravagant teenage queen's demise with wit and humor. Based on the book by Antonia Fraser.

The Other Boleyn Girl

Sisters compete for the attention of King Henry VIII during the Tudor era. Based on the book by Philippa Gregory.

The Suffragette

Follows the working women involved in the early feminist movement. This book will appeal to fans of the graphic novel *Sally Heathcote, Suffragette* by Mary M. Talbot.

War Horse
> When his horse is sold, Albert goes to fight in World War I. Based on the novel by Michael Morpurgo and adapted to the stage by Nick Stafford.

Water for Elephants
> Chronicles a romance set in a traveling circus in the 1930s. Based on the Sara Gruen novel.

Television

Downton Abbey
> Follows a British aristocratic family during the early twentieth century.

Timeless
> Suspenseful sci-fi time travel drama.

The Tudors
> Examines the social and political drama inside the court of King Henry VIII.

Vikings
> Violent historical drama that follows the Viking hero Ragnar Lothbrok.

Recommendations for Readers' Advisory

It is not necessary to be an expert in historical fiction to recommend titles to teens, but it is important to listen to what they are specifically looking for. Does the teen want to learn more about a particular person, era, or topic? Are they looking for action, a mystery, or a romance? Is there a homework requirement they are trying to fulfill? If so, what are the parameters of that assignment?

Focus on the factors that will appeal to teens, like the friendship and tension in *Code Name Verity*, and downplay the "historical fiction" label. Be creative with display areas. Experiment with "if you like this, try that" displays, pairing slower-moving, current-day relationship stories with period romances, or intense dystopian violence with historical war novels. Rick Riordan readers are often looking for a new series to follow, and some of them may enjoy books with paranormal monsters like *Jackaby*.

Many Alex Award winners and nominations have been historical fiction books, so that's a good place to go for recommendations. Exceptional titles noted by the committee include the romance *Water for Elephants,* the historical fantasy *The Watchmaker of Filigree Street,* and the Holocaust story *The Book of Aron.*

Keeping Up with New and Upcoming Titles

Journals

Booklist's annual Historical Fiction issue comes out each April.

Websites

Historical Novel.info: Young Adult Historical Novels: www.historicalnovels.info/Young-Adult-Historical-Novels.html

> A blog covering historical fiction for adults, with a YA section organized by time periods.

Jefferson-Madison Regional Library: www.jmrl.org/wiki/Main_Page

> This Charlottesville, Virginia, library posts diverse lists such as "African American Historical Fiction Novels for Teens" and "Historical Young Adult Fiction around the World" on their wiki.

Reading Rants: Historical Fiction for Hipsters: www.readingrants.org/category/historical-fiction-for-hipsters/

> A reading list of more gripping historical fiction for today's teens—think mysteries, action, and gore.

Awards and Lists

Geoffrey Bilson Award for Historical Fiction for Young Readers: http://bookcentre.ca/programs/awards/geoffrey-bilson-award-for-historical-fiction-for-young-people/

> An award for Canadian literature written for young readers up to age eighteen.

National Jewish Book Award: www.jewishbookcouncil.org/awards/national-jewish-book-award.html

> Outstanding books exploring the Jewish experience. Separate category for young adult literature. The winners are often works of historical fiction.

Scott O'Dell Award for Historical Fiction: http://scottodell.com/
the-scott-odell-award

> Historical fiction award for books written for children or young adults,
> and specifically targeting new authors.

Sydney Taylor Book Award: http://jewishlibraries.org/content.php
?page=Sydney_Taylor_Book_Award

> Books that portray the Jewish experience. Separate category for teens.
> The winners are often works of historical fiction.

Print Resources

Rabey, Melissa. *Historical Fiction for Teens: A Genre Guide.* Santa Barbara,
  CA: Libraries Unlimited, 2011.

Saricks, Joyce. *The Readers' Advisory Guide to Genre Fiction.* 2nd ed.
  Chicago: American Library Association, 2009.

NOTES

1. Jennifer Hubert, *Reading Rants: A Guide to Books That Rock* (New York: Neal-Schuman, 2007), 145.
2. Joyce G. Saricks, *The Readers' Advisory Guide to Genre Fiction,* 2nd ed. (Chicago: American Library Association, 2009), 297.

11

Adrenaline

Mystery, Suspense, Crime, Thriller, Adventure, Supernatural Thriller

This chapter addresses several genres with close ties. Why present them as a group? It is the rare teen who cares about or understands the difference between, say, suspense novels and thrillers. Even librarians use the words "mystery," "thriller," and "suspense" nearly interchangeably in book reviews. Many popular young adult novels blend elements of more than one of these genres. Yet, even given all of the genre-blending that occurs, it is useful for us as readers' advisors to sort out the strands of appeal for each genre. We will define each genre in turn, and it will be easy to see the connections and similarities among them. Even better, picking apart their differences helps to clarify the appeal of each.

Before we do so, it is important to note that we are mixing adventure, suspense, and thrillers with genres that traditionally appeal to the intellect (mysteries and psychological suspense).[1] What makes the mixture work here is that teen fiction simply doesn't hold many examples of pure intellectual appeal within its popular mysteries and psychological suspense titles. Most authors hedge their bets by using suspense and thrills to keep readers moving through the pages. We also include crime novels here, which are popular because they offer readers insight into characters living in the dark underbelly of society.

Finally, we will examine novels that add the supernatural to these genres. We are not talking about paranormal romance, the subgenre that blossomed thanks to Stephenie Meyer's *Twilight*. (This requires a romance between a human and a supernatural creature.) Here we are talking about stories based in reality, with added supernatural elements enhancing the mystery or thriller—teens with psychic powers, for example.

The examples in this chapter are wholly contemporary, which means that historical mysteries and thrillers are to be found in the "Historical Fiction" chapter. And while war books could have landed here, most are set in the past (if not always the distant past), and not all are adrenaline reads. Please see the "Historical Fiction" chapter for those categories.

Genre definitions and appeal are specified at the start of each genre's treatment in this chapter.

Appeal

Consider how frequently mystery, thriller, and suspense elements are found in other genres. We talk about realistic novels with thriller pacing, or we note a mystery at the heart of a story. Several of the titles highlighted in the "Science Fiction" chapter are thrillers. Most of our core horror titles are suspenseful. In this chapter, we examine the appeal elements involved in the purest examples of these adrenaline genres in order to understand just what appeals to teens, even if they are not sure what to call it. Here are some generalizations about the various appeal elements.

Tone

If the books in this chapter had to be summed up in one short phrase, it would be "teens in danger." Whether they are potential victims or strong investigators, our teen protagonists are dealing with unsavory characters and situations that place them in jeopardy. A general atmosphere of menace and uncertainty prevails, whether we are talking about climbing Mount Everest or being bullied by a classmate. Dark and even brutal is acceptable here, but the occasional light-hearted romp of a mystery (by Carl Hiaasen, for example) is also popular.

Pacing

Pacing is the key to the appeal of the books in the adrenaline genres, making them particularly popular with reluctant readers. They feel the impetus to read just one more chapter. That said, crime and mystery plots can be slower to develop, and some readers are happy with a detailed puzzle to solve. Adele Griffin's *The Unfinished Life of Addison Stone* is a good example of a book that never feels slow, yet gives the reader time to pick apart the strands of the victim's unusual life and death.

Characterization

Many of the characters in these books are strong and skilled, and smarter and more talented than average. (Think Jason Bourne or Lisbeth Salander.) Even better, the teen protagonists are often smarter or more intuitive than the adults in their lives. The investigator (mystery) or victim (suspense) is usually appealing and sympathetic, which helps to ground the reader even as the plot may stretch belief.

Story/Theme

One of the ways that adrenaline authors keep their readers hooked is by coming up with unexpected twists and turns of plot. Even if the story is relatively straightforward, the telling rarely is, keeping teens on their toes. Popular devices include going back and forth in time, flashbacks, alternating multiple perspectives, and even starting at the end and moving backwards to the beginning (think *Genuine Fraud* by E. Lockhart). Themes of discovery, secrets, bravery, and justice prevail. Many protagonists end up righting a wrong, escaping bad people, or avenging an injustice.

Setting

Exotic settings are rare in these genres as written for teens; this is quite different from mysteries and thrillers published for adults, in which series are known for taking their readers to international locales. (Clive Cussler and Daniel Silva stand out.) Small towns and everyday life are more common in YA books, perhaps making the menace even more threatening since it hits close to home. Adventure novels are where we find the most emphasis on setting—but these are mostly of the dangerous variety.

Key Genres, Subgenres, and Core Titles

Mystery

In a mystery, a crime is committed and an investigator takes on the case. The investigator (usually the protagonist) interviews and examines a host of secondary characters, trying to find out who did what and why. The story moves relentlessly toward a solution, with the detective solving the puzzle step by step using logic and observation. Among well-known traditional mysteries Agatha Christie remains a favorite, especially with younger teens. Mystery appeals on two main fronts: the joy of methodical detection, and the character of the investigator. In YA novels, solving the crime may reveal surprising connections to the teen detective's own life or family. Most contemporary mysteries play on the reader's emotional connection to the investigator and take on a faster pace, making the reading experience closer to that of a thriller or suspense novel. The BBC's *Sherlock* television series, which is hugely popular with teens, is a great example of a mystery that adopts thriller pacing.

CORE TITLE

Trouble Is a Friend of Mine, by Stephanie Tromly (Arthur Ellis 2016)

This witty mystery is a great example of light-hearted caper humor that is used to leaven two teens' investigation of a serious crime. After Zoe and her mother move to a small New York suburban town, she has trouble making friends at the local high school. She falls in with Digby, who is investigating the disappearance of a classmate because he knows it is related to the disappearance of his sister years earlier. Digby is quite a character—a loner with no patience for social niceties who trusts no one but the new girl; he is a hyper-observant boy who fearlessly breaks into businesses, confronts drug dealers, and gets to the bottom of the crime, dragging Zoe along for the ride. This book has been called a cross between *The Breakfast Club* and *Veronica Mars,* which just about fits. The frequent banter and heightened scenes of high school drama and cliques, and the vivid characters and relationships are the real draws here. The improbable but always entertaining investigation is the motor that keeps it all moving.

NEXT READS

A Study in Charlotte, by Brittany Cavallaro (BFYA 2017)

Fans of BBC's *Sherlock* and CBS's *Elementary* will enjoy this similarly contemporary Holmes reimagining in which Dr. Watson's great-great-great-grandson attends the same Connecticut boarding school as the great-great-great-granddaughter of Sherlock Holmes. James cannot wait to meet Charlotte; he has always imagined the great adventures they would have together. Unfortunately, she does not feels the same. But when they are framed for the murder of a classmate, they end up working together to solve the crime. This book bears many similarities to Conan Doyle's classic tales: it contains references to the original Sherlock stories; a talented but antisocial and possibly drug-addicted Holmes; and a Watson who enjoys writing on the side, and who naturally plays the sidekick. But the possibility of romantic attraction? That's new. This is a steadily paced teen mystery in which the appeal lies in unique characterizations, a darker-than-usual boarding school milieu, and, of course, the solving of the case.

Curious Incident of the Dog in the Night-Time, by Mark Haddon (Alex and BBYA 2003)

This book has been around for many years, and every new audience of teen readers seems to love it just the same. The unique voice of its narrator, fifteen-year-old Christopher, and the extent to which readers come to care for him are at the root of its appeal. Christopher is autistic. He doesn't understand other people very well, he is a math genius, and he has very particular habits, likes, and dislikes, which he lays out in his straightforward, logical manner. When the next-door neighbor's dog is murdered in the front yard, Christopher decides to figure out who did it using the methods and deductive reasoning of one of his favorite characters, Sherlock Holmes. His investigation takes him beyond his daily routines and far from his small English town, where he uncovers a surprising and very personal secret. Readers particularly enjoy the subtle humor that infuses Christopher's narrative.

Finding Nouf, by Zoe Ferraris (Alex 2009)

This first in an adult mystery series stands out for both its investigators and its setting, which affords readers an insider look at gender politics in contemporary Saudi Arabia. Sixteen-year-old Nouf ash-Shrawi's body is found in the desert three days before her wedding. Nayir is a devout Muslim desert guide and family friend who is asked to investigate. He is earnestly determined to help, but feels uncomfortable working with the young female medical examiner assigned to the case, Katya Hijazi. As a devout Muslim, Nayir is not supposed to look at a woman's face, nor speak directly to a single young woman. But he has no choice if he is going to pursue the case. The two investigators slowly become friends, and their relationship changes both of them. The mystery itself is equally intriguing. Did Nouf run away, or was she kidnapped? Was it an accident, or was she murdered? And why?

Suspense

In thrillers and mysteries, the worst has already happened. But in suspense novels, there is a feeling of something menacing *about* to happen. An unexpected danger from an unknown source intrudes into the protagonist's everyday life. The threat appears immediately, even if the plot then goes back and forth in time to build tension. The purest examples of the genre rarely devote time to building up a complicated setting or frame; they lean on atmosphere and tone. It is very important for the reader to empathize with the protagonist in these novels, and the reader probably knows more about just how much danger the protagonist is in than the protagonist himself. Suspense novels can be scary, almost at the level of horror fiction, but without the gore and terror. And here the threat is realistic, rather than supernatural.[2] Teens love the chills that come from reading about other teens in jeopardy. They still enjoy classics like *The Face on the Milk Carton* and *I Know What You Did Last Summer,* while award-winning authors like Kevin Brooks and Stephanie Kuehn have turned their hand to dark new plotlines.

Psychological suspense in particular is popular and trending, thanks to the perpetual fascination with the inner workings of our brains, and especially with minds that function outside the norm. In many of these novels, the popular "unreliable narrator" trope combines with classic psychological suspense attributes like protagonists who question their own sanity, have amnesia, or are full of guilt over something unspoken in their past. The plots are often twisted stories of greed, obsession, guilt, and revenge. These novels may not be fast-paced and may be more literary in style, but all the same, readers often race through them to get to the truth.

CORE TITLE

The Night She Disappeared, by April Henry (PPYA 2015,
QP Top Ten 2013)

> This classic suspense novel begins on the night that teenaged Kayla goes out to make a pizza delivery and doesn't return. Her coworkers Drew, who took the call, and Gabie, another driver, decide to search for Kayla themselves since the police believe she's dead. The book's chapters alternate points of view, and include transcripts of 911 calls and medical reports. Readers even hear from the kidnapper and the victim, so they know that Kayla is still alive. They also feel the suspense ratchet up as the kidnapper decides to kill Kayla and switches

his focus to Gabie. Henry manages to keep the identity of this potential serial killer a mystery, only increasing the sense of menace. An atmospheric contemporary rural setting outside Portland, Oregon, where most of the scenes take place at night, adds to the appeal. The characters are appealing and determined, and the tension never lets up. Kidnapping is a popular trope, and this case is particularly well done—a perfect read for teens who are curious to experience a missing persons investigation from the inside.

NEXT READS

★*We Were Liars*, by E. Lockhart (BFYA 2015)

This quintessential story of psychological suspense takes place on a private island near Cape Cod, where the members of one very wealthy family spend their summers. The patriarch lives in the big house, and his three daughters have more modest houses scattered around the island. Cadence, the daughter of one of these daughters, is one of four "liars" who include her cousins Johnny and Mirren, and their friend Gat. The liars spent summers together from age eight until a tragedy took place during their fifteenth summer. Now it is two years later and Cadence is back on the island for the first time, piecing together what happened through a haze of amnesia. Eventually, the reader realizes that she is an unreliable narrator in the middle of the ultimate dysfunctional family. This story of greed, secrets, and guilt is also a tragic love story with a shocking twist of an ending.

My Sister Rosa, by Justine Larbalestier (BFYA 2017)

Here's one for teens who relish a story laced with menace and foreboding. Seventeen-year-old Che is the only one who understands his sister Rosa, age ten, because he's the only one with whom she shares her thoughts and beliefs. Che is certain that Rosa is a psychopath, and he fears that she will start killing soon. When the family moves from Australia to New York City for their father's work, Che has a lot of changes to handle. He needs to find a new boxing studio, which is his only release from the tension of protecting the world from Rosa, and he falls in love for the first time. Larbalestier also incorporates issues of diversity and privilege. This novel is chilling, thought-provoking,

Young adult books with particular appeal for adult readers are designated with a star (★).

and just plain scary, even as some readers might find doubts nagging in the back of their minds—is Che right about his sister, or is he paranoid?

Rebecca, by Daphne DuMaurier

This classic gothic romantic suspense novel often becomes a lifelong favorite of the teens who discover it, for it is a masterpiece of atmosphere, setting, and sinister tone. The main character is known only as the new Mrs. de Winter. Rebecca was the first wife of Max de Winter, and the second Mrs. de Winter arrives at their home in Cornwall to find that Rebecca's presence still infuses everything. Rebecca's bedroom is still in place, and the house is still run the way she would have had it. This is perhaps because of mysterious and foreboding Mrs. Danvers, the housekeeper who adored Rebecca. The estate of Manderley is a character in itself, with its house and grounds overlooking the sea. At times our protagonist seems in jeopardy for her life, trapped in a life suffused with menace, living with a man who keeps his secrets close. *Rebecca* is a great escape from everyday life, as readers with a penchant for romance and mystery find themselves swept away.

Crime

Crime novels feature young criminal protagonists or the child of a criminal who somehow becomes immersed in the parent's criminal life. They provide an inside look at the life and mind of a criminal, as well as an examination of the fine line between guilt and innocence. Crime novels, which are often some mixture of mystery, suspense, and thriller, can be particularly gritty (think organized crime), but they also encompass humorous caper novels and stories about intriguing con artists. That said, most criminal teen protagonists in YA literature tend to be decent people who are trying to make the best decisions under difficult circumstances. This may be why true crime is just as popular, if not more so, than crime fiction with teens. In true crime, readers get to encounter even darker "stories" in books like Truman Capote's *In Cold Blood* or *The 57 Bus* by Dashka Slater. Also, teen readers have beautifully written, literary adult crime novels with teen appeal to choose from, like *Dodgers* by Bill Beverly or *The Twelve Lives of Samuel Hawley* by Hannah Tinti.

CORE TITLE

Pretending to Be Erica, by Michelle Painchaud (QP 2016, ITW Thriller Award)

> Erica Silverman was kidnapped at age five and killed two weeks later. But only her killer and Sal know that she is dead. Sal adopted Violet out of foster care because she bore an uncanny resemblance to Erica. He groomed her and taught her the skills she would need, especially an ability to manipulate people. A life of crime is all Violet has ever known. As the book opens, she is one month into impersonating Erica, living with Erica's mother and pretending to remember childhood friends. The goal? A painting worth $60 million locked away in a safe in the family library. Sal already has a buyer. Violet just needs to sustain the con long enough to learn the code and steal the painting. But she finds that she likes having a loving mother, and she enjoys going to school and making friends. When she finally gets the chance to steal the painting, she finds herself torn about hurting these people who care about her. This is a thought-provoking novel that is impossible to put down.

NEXT READS

Heist Society, by Ally Carter (PPYA 2013)

> Kat was born into a family of thieves, but by the time she turns sixteen she's ready to get out of the business. Then her father gets into deep trouble for stealing from the wrong man. Arturo Taccone does not play games, and he wants his paintings returned. Unfortunately, Kat's father wasn't the one who stole them. The only way to help him is to find out who did and steal the paintings back. Kat and her friend Hale gather a team and set off to, rather glamorously, jet around the world getting the job done. Hale is a billionaire sixteen-year-old with whom Kat slowly but surely falls in love along the way. The heist turns serious when they discover that the paintings were stolen by Nazis during World War II. This series will appeal to readers looking for something light-hearted yet daring—even the criminal protagonists have good intentions.

Fake ID, by Lamar Giles (QP 2015)

> Nick is a young African American teen who has lived in the witness protection program (WITSEC) with his family for four years. His father was an accountant to a mobster, and he still refuses to go straight even

though his activities endanger his family. The government is losing patience; this placement in a small southern town is the family's last chance. On the first day at his new school, Nick is shown around by Eli Cruz, who recruits him into the journalism club, and Nick develops a crush on Eli's beautiful sister Reya. After Eli mentions something named "Whispertown," he is found dead. Nick investigates, encountering deep issues of loyalty and trust. This mystery involves a government conspiracy, a surprising betrayal by WITSEC itself, major character deaths, and an unexpected villain. The twists and revelations keep coming, making this book ideal for readers who like to be kept guessing and are up for its grittiness.

The Lock Artist, by Steve Hamilton (Alex 2011, Dagger Award, Edgar Award)

This character-based novel follows Mike, who became mute after a traumatic event when he was eight. Now he's nine years into a prison term and ready to write his story. Mike's narrative flashes from the present back to his first professional job four months shy of his eighteenth birthday. Then to his junior year of high school, when he discovers a natural talent for picking locks and ends up on probation, entrusted to Mr. Marsh, a man who owes a debt to a serious group of criminals. The novel's shifting back and forth in time draws out the suspense, particularly concerning Mike's relationship with Mr. Marsh's daughter, Amelia, how he ended up in prison, and the event that caused him to be mute. Mike is likable and sympathetic, and he shares a fascinating insider's look at lock-picking and safecracking, and the criminal world he was forced to navigate.

Thriller

Thrillers are plot-centered, fast-paced novels in which action dominates. A protagonist finds herself in a threatening situation and she doesn't know who to trust. The reader sympathizes, but a thriller is less about character development and more about the skills the protagonist possesses that help her to survive, escape the situation, or ensure that justice is done. The plots are full of twists and turns, conspiracies and secrets that keep reluctant readers glued to the page. This genre also appeals for its cool technology—panic rooms, weaponry, forensics, and codes among them. Adult thrillers separate out into conspiracy, espionage, cyber, medical, and legal subgenres.[3] (Think John Grisham or Dan Brown.) Teen thrillers are less defined, and are full of self-sufficient young people whose abilities approach that of a superhero. Spy thrillers belong here, but unlike the ever-popular *Alex Rider*, *Young Bond*, and *Gallagher Girls* series that cater more to middle grade readers, teen spies are plagued by issues of identity and purpose. The trickle-down effect of the popularity of Stieg Larsson's *Millennium Trilogy* shows up in this genre.

CORE TITLE

★*The City of Saints & Thieves,* by Natalie C. Anderson (BFYA 2018)

Tina follows strict, self-developed rules in order to survive living homeless on the streets of (fictional) Sangui City, Kenya. She is planning the destruction of Mr. Greyhill, the powerful and wealthy man who killed her mother. Tina uses her connections with a street gang (and the hacker who is the closest thing she has to a friend) to get inside the house, the same house where she and her mother lived until her mother's murder. She is caught in the act by Greyhill's son, Michael, a childhood playmate and friend, and the novel takes off. The pace never slows, even while incorporating human rights and gender equality issues and the imbalance of wealth and poverty in an area of the world that is wrestling with war and colonialism. Tina must travel to remote Congo, which her mother fled years before, to find the surprising answer to the mystery of her death. Tina has focused her whole being on revenge—but what if she was wrong? Teens will love this determined, independent girl who overcomes so much in her quest for justice.

NEXT READS

You Don't Know My Name, by Kristen Orlando

Seventeen-year-old Reagan is the daughter of two operatives with the Black Angels, a covert government agency, and she's been training to follow in their footsteps since the age of ten. After constantly relocating to maintain their cover, they've been living in small-town Ohio for over a year, and Reagan is beginning to imagine what life *could* be outside the "prison" of parental expectations. She's also becoming close to a handsome neighbor. But what about her panic attacks and paranoia? Is she imagining the van casing their house, or the school janitor who watches her too intensely? Unfortunately not, and Reagan plunges into a reckless mission to rescue her parents from a

Colombian drug lord. This book is a terrific suggestion for readers who want more than pure adrenaline in their thrillers. The longer-than-usual buildup to the action pays off in emotional engagement, and includes enough panic rooms and weaponry to keep spy-loving teens very entertained.

I Hunt Killers, by Barry Lyga (BFYA, QP Top Ten 2013; PPYA 2015)

Meet Jasper "Jazz" Dent, the teenaged son of convicted serial killer, Billy Dent. Jazz is determined to use the skills his father taught him (pre-incarceration) to investigate a series of murders that copycat his father's pattern. Billy exposed him to his work at a young age, even putting Jazz in charge of trophies—the items he took from each of his victims. While Jazz has great respect for Sheriff G. William Tanner, the man who ended his father's killing spree, he needs to solve the murders quickly in order to avoid the suspicion that might naturally fall his way. This is a dark, gory thriller with heavy elements of forensic science and mystery. It also has a sense of humor. Jazz and his only friend, Howie, make joking references to popular television series like *CSI*, as well as serial killers in pop culture. This is the first book in a trilogy that has received acclaim throughout.

Reconstructing Amelia, by Kimberly McCreight

This is an adult mixture of a murder mystery and a legal thriller with plenty of teen appeal. Single mother Kate is called to come pick up her fifteen-year-old daughter Amelia from school. She has been suspended for cheating. But by the time Kate arrives, Amelia is dead; she has flung herself from the roof of the school. Or has she? Kate begins receiving anonymous text messages intimating that Amelia was murdered. Kate is a litigation attorney and a partner in her law firm, and she insists on teaming up with the police detective in charge of her daughter's case and joining the investigation. The novel alternates between daughter and mother, past and present, taking the reader through the twists and turns of Amelia's last weeks using blog and social media posts, e-mails and text messages in a harrowing story of bullying, secret societies, and revenge. The pace never flags on its way to a surprising ending.

Adventure

Adventure novels are centered on adrenaline, survival, action, and endurance. They have a lot in common with thrillers, but here the natural world is the principal threat. Many young adult books in this genre are about surviving a natural disaster or an accident that strands a teen in the natural world. (Gary Paulsen's *Hatchet* is a classic example.) Adventure is pure escapism. The protagonists have to bring out the very best in themselves to survive, and teens find it exciting and satisfying to put themselves in the mind or place of someone their age who is smart and talented enough to make it out alive. Like thrillers, these stories are often about *doing*, rather than feeling or thinking. School days and other everyday situations are few and far between in these stories. Strong adventure elements are found in other genres, too. Dystopian and post-apocalyptic books are full of disaster survival, and even readers who shy away from historical fiction read the *Bloody Jack Adventures* by L. A. Meyer. There are several nonfiction classics that appeal to adventure readers, like *127 Hours: Between a Rock and a Hard Place* and *The Perfect Storm*. In fact, many teen adventure readers prefer true stories to fiction.

CORE TITLE

Peak, by Roland Smith (BBYA and QP 2008; PPYA 2012)

This is as close as fiction gets to the experience of reading the (nonfictional) Mount Everest disaster story *Into Thin Air.* When he is caught climbing Manhattan skyscrapers, Peak dodges a juvenile detention sentence by leaving the country to live with Josh, his estranged father and rock-climbing superstar. Little does he know that Josh has a plan to make fourteen-year-old Peak the youngest person ever to reach the summit of Mount Everest—and save his business in the process. Peak is surrounded by people with mysterious hidden agendas, from Zopa, a retired Sherpa assigned to deliver Peak to the Everest base camp, to Peak's new friend and rival Sun-jo. The dangers and rewards of climbing Everest, as well as the risks taken by Sherpas in order to make a living, are depicted in heart-stopping fashion. Smith integrates enough technical detail to make teens feel like they are reading about the real thing. Told from Peak's point of view, this book is perfect for adventurers and reluctant readers. The release of a 2015 sequel, *The Edge,* put this favorite back into high circulation.

NEXT READS

Adrift, by Paul Griffin

Matt and Dree meet by chance on a Long Island beach, and the next night Matt goes to a party at her parents' mansion. When Dree's cousin Estefania goes windsurfing in bad weather, Matt and his best friend John, Dree, and Estefania's boyfriend JoJo go out in a small boat to bring her in before she gets hurt. She gets hurt and worse, and her would-be rescuers end up drifting far from land, fighting to survive for days at sea under the August sun. At first they work together, but everyone on board brings their own personal demons. This book is a heavy read, but it's never slow. The attraction between Matt and Dree is perhaps ill-fated, but is all the more poignant for how deep it goes between two truly good people. This book is much more than a survival story, since class, race, and psychological issues become as critical as water and food.

Those Who Wish Me Dead, by Michael Koryta (Alex 2015)

This adult thriller follows Ethan Serbin, an Air Force veteran turned survival instructor based in the Montana mountains, and the teen boy he agrees to protect. In an unforgettable opening sequence, Jace Wilson is quarry-jumping alone when he finds a dead body, and then witnesses a second murder by two terrifying, creepy, and violent men, the Blackwell Brothers. The Brothers pursue Jace through the woods, but he manages to escape them. Later, after a close call in the witness protection program, Jace is placed in a group of teen delinquents taking Ethan's summer course. The narrative is filled with fascinating instruction about wilderness survival, and Jace shows a real aptitude for Ethan's teaching. This is a good thing, because the Brothers are close behind, setting the forest on fire to smoke out their prey. The tension of this cat-and-mouse game never lets up, including some outstanding twists.

Girl Underwater, by Claire Kells

Avery is a long-distance competitive swimmer and a sophomore at Stanford University when the plane she's taking home from school crashes in the Rocky Mountains. Only Avery, her teammate Colin, and three young boys survive. They spend five terrible days in the wilderness facing severe cold, snowstorms, and a bear attack. On the fifth day, something happens that makes Avery so ashamed that she cannot visit the boys or Colin after their rescue. She even lies to the media. Alternating chapters between the event and its aftermath ramp up the suspense concerning the details of the tragedy and Avery's subsequent struggle with post-traumatic stress disorder. Avery is strong and flawed; teen readers will love her deeply emotional, and at times anxiety-ridden story. Colin is a truly good man, a humble hero to make readers swoon. This adult survival novel has the pacing of a thriller, elements of psychological suspense, and the heart of a romance.

Supernatural Mysteries and Thrillers

The supernatural brings unpredictability and goosebumps to a mystery or thriller, expanding its possibilities beyond the everyday while staying within the expectations of the genre. This combination is hugely popular with teen readers. The subgenre's tropes include a detective or investigator with special abilities, a "normal" investigator who discovers that the solution to the mystery involves the supernatural, or psychological suspense that includes magical or supernatural elements. Teens with special powers or abilities are particularly popular, everything from seeing into the future or other people's dreams to moving objects without touching them. Most protagonists in this subgenre are female.

CORE TITLE

★*The Walls Around Us*, by Nova Ren Suma (BFYA 2016)

This outstanding novel of psychological suspense alternates the stories of two girls. Violet (Vee) is performing in her last recital before leaving for Juilliard. Amber is incarcerated in a juvenile detention center, where one stormy night the power goes out and the cell doors open. In the middle of the ensuing confusion, Amber witnesses a girl entering the prison, a ghost wandering into a place where she doesn't belong. Who is she? And why does Amber feel like this has all happened before? Returning to Vee, the reader learns about her best friend Orianna, who was top ballerina in their studio until three years before when two girls were murdered during a performance. How are these girls connected? The author keeps her readers off balance with mesmerizing, almost dreamlike writing. Hints of the supernatural blossom at the end when some, but not all, of the story's mysteries are solved. Readers who are comfortable with the unexplained and are attracted to the darker side of female friendships, rivalries, and violence are the target audience.

NEXT READS

Scarlett Undercover, by Jennifer Latham (QP 2016)

What begins as a traditional murder mystery with an intriguing teen detective evolves into a battle between good and evil. Scarlett is an orphaned Muslim teen who tested out of high school and started her own investigation company. When a young girl comes to her fearful for (and of) her older brother, Scarlett quickly connects the case to an artifact from the time of King Solomon. It takes her a couple more steps to realize that she is right in the middle of a continuing war between her own family, their allies, and rivals who believe themselves to be descended from the jinn (genies). This novel juxtaposes its supernatural elements with a gritty urban setting that is firmly in our world. The plot moves at a steady pace as Scarlett discovers each piece of the puzzle while being threatened at every turn. Readers who enjoy a strong, sympathetic female protagonist are the ideal audience.

The Runner, by Patrick Lee

This is an exemplary "military experiment gone wrong" conspiracy techno-thriller, with a twist. Sam Dryden is out jogging in the middle of the night when he collides with a young teen running for her life. For the last several weeks, Rachel has been held in a laboratory where she was restrained, drugged, and questioned. That night her captors decided to kill her, so she escaped. And Rachel can read minds. Actually, reading minds is not her only power, but she cannot remember anything before her time in the lab. Dryden is former military, an elite black ops Delta Ranger. He vows to keep her safe until the drugs wear off and her memory returns. Martin Gaul works for a corporation that is experimenting with genetic manipulation for the government. It is crucial that Rachel dies before their latest project goes live. Either way, the world is about to change. The action is breathtaking, with a climactic ending in which Rachel's powers are on full display.

Lexicon, by Max Barry (Alex 2014)

In this adult thriller, power resides in using the right words to control minds and actions. Sixteen-year-old Emily Ruff uses her talent with words to survive on the streets of San Francisco, conning anyone foolish enough to engage with her. Her potential gets her an invitation from a secret international organization to train as a "poet." It turns out that she's a prodigy, so good at reading personalities and finding the words to control people that she is asked to leave under mysterious circumstances. In a parallel story, the only survivor of a mass violent incident in Australia is kidnapped and interrogated, even though he's lost his memory. How are these two connected? This novel is funny, violent, and tragic, at times madcap, and at other times terrifying in its twists and turns. It even holds a sweet love story. The pace is fast and the ideas whip-smart, encompassing privacy and fake news.

Expanding Readers' Horizons into the Whole Collection

Movies

The Bourne Identity

This series based on the Robert Ludlum novels features an international assassin who has lost his memory.

Get Out

This one may be closer to horror, but deserves mention here for its psychological suspense and murder elements.

The Girl with the Dragon Tattoo

Based on the novel by Stieg Larsson, this features the ruthless yet sympathetic computer hacker Lisbeth Salander.

In the Heart of the Sea

This historical nonfiction film hits all the appeal triggers of contemporary adventure. A New England ship is sunk by a giant whale.

James Bond movies

The ultimate spy thrillers based on novels by Ian Fleming.

Mission Impossible

This series of thrillers features an unstoppable agent and plenty of cutting-edge technology.

Ocean's Eleven

Excellent heist film with older stars that teens still recognize.

Shutter Island

Teens love Leonardo DiCaprio, and this is an excellent example of psychological suspense and an unreliable narrator.

The Silence of the Lambs

This crime thriller is the best of the best in serial killer films.

The Usual Suspects

A perfect heist movie featuring the ultimate unreliable narrator.

Television

Bones

> This is based on the Temperance Brennan mysteries by Kathy Reichs, and both the forensic science and the romantic chemistry draw teens.

Law & Order

> This war horse, the original series rather than its spin-offs, is still popular with teen viewers in reruns.

Pretty Little Liars

> Based on the series by Sara Shepard.

Riverdale

> A dark, contemporary crime series based on Archie Comics in which a teen is murdered on the 4th of July and the small-town residents investigate.

Sherlock

> This BBC reboot starring Benedict Cumberbatch brings Holmes and Watson into the twenty-first century.

Thirteen Reasons Why

> Based on the novel by Jay Asher, this Netflix adaptation received criticism for its treatment of suicide but is nevertheless hugely popular with teens.

Veronica Mars

> Veronica is the ultimate teen detective who started out assisting her private-eye father. First a television series, then a movie, and currently a book series by Rob Thomas.

Recommendations for Readers' Advisory

Knowing the shorthand involved with each genre's most popular examples can be a lifesaver when communicating with teen patrons. Watching one season of *Veronica Mars* or BBC's *Sherlock*, and reading *We Were Liars* or an April Henry teen suspense novel can take our ability to suggest read-alikes to a new level. *Gone Girl* and *The Girl on the Train* may seem too risqué for teens, but they are reading and loving them and are looking for more. It helps to keep an eye on the latest hot adult novel at these high popularity levels. (A movie deal is a major clue.)

Several best-selling adult authors write mystery and thriller series for young people, including Harlan Coben (*Mickey Bolitar* novels), John Grisham (*Theodore Boone* series), Kathy Reichs (*Virals* novels), James Patterson (*Confessions* series), Anthony Horowitz (*Alex Rider* series), and Elizabeth George (*Whidbey Island* series). Teens, especially older teens, are as likely to read these authors' adult series, however. When at a loss to suggest a YA book to a teen seeking a mystery or thriller, it is just as effective to offer an adult favorite, even if it is a few years old.

Young adults who miss the long series they enjoyed when they were younger[4] may find the same satisfaction in adult series like Laurie King's *Mary Russell* novels, the *Maisie Dobbs* series by Jacqueline Winspear, or Alan Bradley's *Flavia de Luce* books. Humorous caper novels are also popular, with witty dialogue propelling clever twists and turns of plot. *The Spellman Files* and Spencer Quinn's *Chet and Bernie* mysteries are favorites.

Keeping Up with New and Upcoming Titles

Journals

Booklist publishes its Mystery Showcase issue on May 1 each year. This issue always offers a list of the year's best crime novels, and often emphasizes another related genre that is trending, too.

Websites

"All About Mysteries for Teens," by Heather Booth. Novelist Plus (accessed Sept. 15, 2018)

The Big Thrill newsletter (International Thriller Writers): www.thebigthrill.org/

Stop You're Killing Me: www.stopyourekillingme.com/
 Good resource for adult mysteries.

Awards and Lists

Agatha Awards: http://malicedomestic.org/agathas.html
 The Malice Domestic website honors traditional mysteries, and includes a Children/Young Adult category.

Anthony Awards: www.bouchercon.com/anthony-awards/
winners-and-nominees/

> Awarded at the annual Bouchercon World Mystery Convention; includes a juvenile/young adult category, though not every year.

Arthur Ellis Awards: www.crimewriterscanada.com/awards/
arthur-ellis-awards/

> Canadian crime writing, includes a Juvenile/YA category.

Dagger Awards: https://thecwa.co.uk/the-daggers/

> Given by the (British) Crime Writers Association for excellence in crime writing and thrillers.

Edgar Awards: www.theedgars.com/

> Sponsored by the Mystery Writers of America, with a category for juvenile mysteries and another for young adult mysteries.

Thriller Awards: http://thrillerwriters.org/programs/award
-nominees-and-winners/

> Sponsored by International Thriller Writers; includes a Young Adult Novel category.

Print Resources

Alessio, Amy J. *Mind-Bending Mysteries and Thrillers for Teens: A Programming and Readers' Advisory Guide*. Chicago: American Library Association, 2014.

Charles, John, Candace Clark, Joanne Hamilton-Selway, and Joanna Morrison. *The Readers' Advisory Guide to Mystery*. 2nd ed. Chicago: American Library Association, 2012.

Saricks, Joyce. *The Readers' Advisory Guide to Genre Fiction*. 2nd ed. Chicago: American Library Association, 2009.

NOTES

1. Joyce G. Saricks, *The Readers' Advisory Guide to Genre Fiction*, 2nd ed. (Chicago: American Library Association, 2009).
2. Ibid, 51.
3. Ibid, 74.
4. Amy J. Alessio, *Mind-Bending Mysteries and Thrillers for Teens: A Programming and Readers' Advisory Guide* (Chicago: American Library Association, 2014), 4.

12

Nonfiction

For teens, the world of nonfiction includes their textbooks, the books they are likely required to use for research projects, the book on display about the Vietnam War that caught their eye while they were lounging in their library's comfy chairs, and the manual on welding that their father asked them to bring home for a home improvement project. Teens are a curious bunch, and they often pursue their interests by reading about them.

Even teens who don't think of themselves as enjoying nonfiction likely read it. They pick up a magazine to learn about hot cars, or they enjoy the browsing collections that are popular in many libraries. These are full of puzzle and joke books, Lego and Minecraft guides, sports statistics, *Ripley's Believe It or Not* and the *Guinness Book of World Records*, fashion, hair and makeup guides, astrology books, and cookbooks. These books satisfy teens' curiosity in quick, easily digestible chunks.

As Neal Wyatt has observed, there are two main types of nonfiction, task books and nontask books.[1] Task books are about learning to do something. For example, how to begin building a world in Minecraft. Nontask books are those that readers turn to for much the same reasons they pick up a novel: for enjoyment, immersion, story, character, language, and detail. Most of the works discussed in this chapter will be these nontask books, which Wyatt also calls narrative nonfiction, or nonfiction that "reads like a novel."[2] If a patron needs a book about creating jewelry (a task book), a simple online catalog search will usually suffice. But if a reader is looking for a narrative nonfiction book of true adventure on the ocean, a librarian can help to identify whether he is interested in the past or present, science or history, sharks or pirates, as well as the kind of reading experience he wants, matching appeal to subject. It is these nontask books that we will focus on in this chapter.

Narrative nonfiction published for a YA audience has become more widely available in the last decade, providing teens with more options than ever. This type of nonfiction used to be the purview of adult books with teen appeal (think of *Into Thin Air* by Jon Krakauer or *Autobiography of a Face* by Lucy Grealy). Then authors like Steve Sheinkin, Deborah Heiligman, and Candace Fleming began writing young adult nonfiction to rival the best adult titles, bringing out the angles of historical stories that are relevant to young people today, and trusting teens to read and enjoy a text without relying on busy sidebars to enhance it.

Overwhelmingly, the most widely read nonfiction for teens is about people, and especially memoirs. But teens also enjoy autobiography and biography geared to their interests. One need look no further than Ron Chernow's *Alexander Hamilton,* over 800 pages long and still checked out by middle school students hoping to learn more about their favorite character from history. Graphic memoirs are especially popular. From personal stories that point up an important moment in history (think of *Maus* and, later, *Persepolis*), we now have *My Friend Dahmer* by Derf Backderf, *Honor Girl* by Maggie Thrash, and *Relish* by Lucy Knisley, which speak directly to teens' interests.

Appeal

To help teens find appealing narrative nonfiction, keep in mind that its readers are just as invested in story, character, setting, and style as fiction readers are. They just happen to love reading about actual events and people. They seek books that bring the real world alive, whether through the mixture of relationships and history in Marc Aronson and Marina Budhos's *Eyes of the World,* or the journalistic account of a shocking crime in Dashka Slater's *The 57 Bus.*

Accuracy is crucial to appeal. Readers need to trust the authors of the books they choose. They may also want to read more on a subject, since teens can become obsessive in their interests. Back matter is where the author proves her chops and directs readers to further information.

More and more frequently, authors present a note within the back matter, explaining their approach to the sources, and especially primary sources. For example, in an engaging preface to her bibliography at the end of *The Family Romanov,* Candace Fleming explains how she chose quotes and how her own travels to Russia informed the book.

Teens especially enjoy memoirs and autobiographies, where they can learn about a person's life from his or her own mouth, so to speak. And reading about people is a gateway to learning about the world. For some, it is more appealing to read Trevor Noah's *Born a Crime* than it is to read a history of apartheid in South Africa.

The Core and Next Reads titles in this chapter are organized into types of nonfiction that are popular with teen readers, chosen with regard to the following appeal elements.

Tone

Each book has its own voice, and a great author finds the perfect tone to match his subject matter. Is the reader looking for a carefully objective and balanced history such as *This Strange Wilderness* by Nancy Plain? Or does she seek an author who writes to persuade her readers to care, like Tanya Lee Stone in *Almost Astronauts* or *Girl Rising?* Is the reader seeking the thrill and drama of *Samurai Rising?* Or the light yet sincere tone of Maya Van Wagenen's *Popular: Vintage Wisdom for a Modern Geek*? That said, teens may not be ready to articulate the tone they are seeking; they are much more likely to ask for a book on a particular topic.

Characterization

Character development is crucial to the appeal of nonfiction. The best authors make their subjects come alive by writing about their development as they age, tracing the changes they experience due to the events of the narrative. And the huge popularity of memoir, autobiography, and biography is largely thanks to readers' interest in what makes other people tick.

Story/Theme

The "plot" of a nonfiction book may not be its true subject. Events are carefully chosen, and the telling is organized to bring the theme to light. Most teens need and expect a strong storyline in narrative nonfiction in order to keep their reading momentum strong. Some nonfiction authors use fiction techniques to accomplish this. They take the story back and forth in time to generate suspense or to highlight cause and effect. Others proceed in chronological order, but use alternate perspectives to hold on to a reader's attention. A memoir may begin with a crucial moment, then back up to show how the author ended up there. (*The Glass Castle* by Jeannette Walls is a classic example.)

Pacing

Pacing in nonfiction varies widely, and illustrations may play a role in helping a book move quickly, or inviting readers to slow down and immerse themselves in the pictures. If readers are stopping to look at period photographs, for example, the narrative is interrupted. But it is not necessarily slowed down. Rather, it could be propelled forward by full-page illustrations that have the reader flipping forward, giving her a sense of motion and accomplishment. Gail Jarrow does this in *Fatal Fever: Tracking Down Typhoid Mary* by using large photographs and tabloid-style chapter headings. Alternatively, in *The Borden Murders,* Sarah Miller lays out primary source documents and ephemera and asks her readers to puzzle through the case. And one of the joys of reading *Some Writer!* by Melissa Sweet is in poring over the details of the illustrations. Perhaps it is more fitting to ask a reader what subject she is interested in, and consider whether she likes to immerse herself in details or race through a thrilling narrative of events.

Setting

Teens are naturally curious about places around the world and other periods of history. They enjoy clear and vivid descriptions that help them picture the setting about which they are reading. In *Enchanted Air,* Margarita Engle uses the contrast of two very different locations, Los Angeles and Cuba, to communicate her childhood feeling of being torn between two homes. In nonfiction illustrated with photographs or other images, the words and pictures work together to place the reader in the moment, perhaps requiring fewer descriptive passages to satisfy the reader's imagination.

Key Subgenres and Core Titles in Nonfiction

Biography

While biography may be a genre that teens encounter in school assignments, that doesn't dim their enthusiasm for reading about other people's lives. Some of the best and brightest young adult authors—and the most highly awarded young adult nonfiction titles—fall into the category of biography, making the possibilities particularly rich. Given that the subjects of narrative nonfiction biography are mostly historical, authors find ways to make these lives relevant to today's teens. The best authors choose their subjects well, finding something within their lives that resonates, while using original research and appropriate graphic elements to tailor the story to teens.

CORE TITLE

Most Dangerous: Daniel Ellsberg and the Secret History of the Vietnam War, by Steve Sheinkin (YALSA Nonfiction Award, Horn Book Award, NBA finalist 2016)

Sheinkin chooses Daniel Ellsberg as the focal point for a narrative of the United States' involvement in the Vietnam War. Ellsberg trained as a Marine, then worked for the Pentagon, where he witnessed how President Lyndon Johnson manipulated the truth he presented to the American people and continued to escalate the war even while more and more citizens began to oppose it. Sheinkin takes readers into combat in Vietnam, and into the "Hanoi Hilton" POW camp with captured U.S. bomber pilots. He shares the antics of the loose cannons G. Gordon Liddy and Howard Hunt, and he guides readers through the Watergate Scandal and President Nixon's eventual resignation. He traces Ellsberg's transformation into an antiwar advocate who was willing to take potentially treasonous action in order to end the war. Sheinkin shows great respect for his readers by presenting complex material, giving them a window into events whose themes continue to echo today. It all culminates in a chapter that compares Edward Snowden's actions to Ellsberg's. Teens feel like they are on the front lines of history, thanks to copious quotes from the players themselves.

NEXT READS

Samurai Rising: The Epic Life of Minamoto Yoshitsune, by Pamela S.
Turner (YALSA Nonfiction Finalist 2017)

> Minamoto Yoshitsune was born into the middle of a bloody civil
> war in the Japanese capital of Kyoto in 1160. Turner hooks her read-
> ers with the night Yoshitsune's father was assassinated (beheaded!)
> for kidnapping the Retired Emperor. At age fifteen, Yoshitsune ran
> away to train as a samurai. Six years later, he fled headlong into war.
> His daring decisions in the heat of battle quickly made him famous—
> plunging down a sheer mountainside to infiltrate enemy fortifica-
> tions, or attacking ships from the backs of horses swimming in stormy
> seas. Turner integrates the political rivalries and daily life and ritu-
> als of early samurai culture into the most famous action sequences of
> Yoshitsune's life, providing details about weapons, armor, honorable
> death, and the high cost of sibling rivalry. Turner maintains historical
> authenticity in the midst of a nonfiction book that reads like a thriller.

★*Vincent and Theo: The Van Gogh Brothers,* by Deborah Heiligman
(Horn Book Award 2017, Printz Honor and YALSA Nonfiction
Award 2018)

> This unique dual biography follows Vincent van Gogh and his brother
> Theo through the periods of their lives as if touring the rooms of an
> art gallery. Many teens can picture Vincent's painting style, or at least
> they have heard about the "crazy" artist who cut off his own ear. But
> this book gives readers an intimate, nuanced story of two very dif-
> ferent men, interdependent brothers, told largely in their own words
> thanks to heavy use of the letters they wrote to each other. Examples
> of Vincent's sketches introduce each new section, and Heiligman pres-
> ents each in a different writing style to match his work. This deeply
> emotional book is an outstanding suggestion for teens fascinated by
> the relationship between mental illness and art, by sibling relation-
> ships, or by Post-Impressionist painting. Short chapters beckon the
> reader to finish just one more about these siblings' tragic lives.

Unbroken: A World War II Story of Survival, Resilience, and Redemption,
by Laura Hillenbrand

> Louie Zamperini's life story is an inspiring modern biography that is
> equally popular with teens and with adults. It is well-paced, engagingly

---

Young adult books with particular appeal for adult readers are designated with a star (★).

told, and encompasses several elements that appeal to young adult readers. Zamperini's coming of age (when he seemed destined to be a petty criminal) leads into the drama of competing in the 1936 Berlin Olympics. Serving as an airman in World War II, he survived forty-seven days on the Pacific Ocean in a raft after his plane went down, and then he was captured and tortured in a Japanese POW camp. While inspiring, this adult book is also graphic and at times difficult to read, but the teens who love it are obsessed with it. A 2014 young reader's edition, subtitled "An Olympian's Journey from Airman to Castaway to Captive," is available for those who desire a less graphic version.

Memoir and Autobiography

Both memoirs and autobiographies are typically first-person narratives about the author's own life and experiences. A memoir typically focuses on intense and meaningful periods in the author's life, while autobiography is defined as a life history written by its subject. Memoirs are incredibly popular with teens, who are drawn to their intimacy and raw honesty. The autobiographies popular with this age group focus on the coming-of-age years, especially of celebrities. Teens are also drawn to humorous essays by writers like David Sedaris and Lena Dunham, whose personalities and experiences seem larger than life. What is the most popular subject matter in this genre? Dysfunctional families, mental or physical health issues, addiction, and abuse, as well as inspiring personal triumphs.

CORE TITLE

The Glass Castle, by Jeannette Walls (Alex 2006; PPYA 2015)

This memoir about a dysfunctional family begins with Walls, a successful writer, looking out a car window to see her mother picking trash from a dumpster—and pretending not to know her. Walls grew up the youngest of three children of an alcoholic father and a self-absorbed, artistic mother who were, at times, criminally neglectful as they moved the family from the Arizona desert to deep poverty in the hills of West Virginia. Walls was smart and resilient even as a child, and no matter what her parents' failings were, she loved them and she knew that they loved her. The siblings balanced fending for themselves and protecting each other, and eventually escaped to New York City. Walls writes brilliantly, forgivingly as a naive child, and more realistically as her teenaged eyes are opened. Her parents are compelling—storytellers, inventors, dreamers, with some mental illness mixed in. This is a character-driven narrative in which the settings are vividly rendered. It is the deeply felt testament of a survivor. This adult memoir's popularity with teens has barely faded in the years since publication, and the 2017 movie only helped to boost its popularity.

NEXT READS

★*March Trilogy,* by John Lewis, Andrew Aydin, and Nate Powell
(*March 3:* NBA 2016; Printz Award, GGNT Top Ten, YALSA Nonfiction Award 2017)

> *March Book 1, March Book 2,* and *March Book 3* comprise a graphic memoir of John Lewis's life, beginning with his childhood growing up on a farm, and ending with the Selma March and the passing of the 1965 Voting Rights Act. The trilogy is inspiring, informative, and infuriating, and is an excellent example of the popular trend of graphic memoirs for teen readers. The black-and-white illustrations are electric, which helps to prevent the story from bogging down when it becomes complex, and it does. Lewis details the inner struggles, as well as the outer battles, of the Civil Rights Movement from his perspective. The cumulative power of Lewis's story could not be more relevant to life today, and teens feel its importance in their own lives.

Bossypants, by Tina Fey

> Comedian Fey's warm, self-deprecating, yet sharp and revealing humor goes down easily in her autobiography, which is presented as a series of short pieces about everything from her nerdy high school years to playing Sarah Palin on *Saturday Night Live,* crushing on Alex Baldwin during *30 Rock,* and experiencing the pitfalls of motherhood. Teens may not enjoy the parenting sections as much as the subtly feminist essays about body image or being a successful woman in the male-dominated world of television and film, but it is easy to skip around in this quick-moving book. Fey is hugely likable, and presents herself as just a normal person who somehow became famous. *Bossypants* is very funny, but it is also insightful, and it continues to be one of the most popular celebrity autobiographies. Fey narrates the audiobook version, which is very entertaining.

The Terrorist's Son: A Story of Choice, by Zak Ebrahim with Jeff Giles
(Alex 2015, QP 2016)

> Ebrahim is the son of the Islamic terrorist El Sayyid Nosair, who was tried but acquitted (when Ebrahim was seven) of the assassination

of Rabbi Meir Kahane, but was sentenced to prison on other charges. Then, from prison, Nosair helped to organize the 1993 World Trade Center bombing. Nosair's actions threw his family into a life of poverty and insecurity. But Ebrahim also believes that it rescued him from living with a father who was intent on teaching him to hate. Instead, Ebrahim embraced peace, empathy, and tolerance, even in the midst of vicious bullying that made him consider suicide. In this memoir, he grapples with understanding what drew his father toward terrorism, and he makes it clear that everyone has a choice to turn away from hate. This book is a powerful, raw, honest account and was originally a TED Talk that was expanded and adapted for print.

Adrenaline Reads

Many readers seek out fictional adrenaline reads, whether thrillers or suspense novels, while others prefer their action and adventure to be based in truth. Armchair teen adventurers can live vicariously, surviving a natural disaster with Jon Krakauer in *Into Thin Air,* pushing the limits of historical investigation in the depths of the ocean in Robert Kurson's *Shadow Divers,* or competing in the Olympics with Daniel Brown's *The Boys in the Boat.* We need more young adult authors to pursue this type of nonfiction; most teen favorites in this category were published for adults.

CORE TITLE

The Nazi Hunters: How a Team of Spies and Survivors Captured the World's Most Notorious Nazi, by Neal Bascomb (YALSA Nonfiction Award 2014)

Adolf Eichmann was in charge of rounding up Jews across Europe and transporting them to the extermination camps during the Holocaust. At the end of World War II, he obtained fake papers and escaped to Argentina, leaving his family behind. This is the story of how he was found and brought to trial in Israel. The web of investigation that resulted in his 1960 capture reads like a spy novel, moving across decades and continents. The reader comes to know the most pathetic of Holocaust victims, the most determined of survivors (including Simon Wiesenthal), and the most dedicated of Mossad spies, as well as one ordinary family in Buenos Aires who suspected they had met Eichmann's son and, fortunately, followed up on that suspicion. Bascomb uses primary source photographs and quotes as he builds a detailed, yet perfectly paced depiction of the capture of a notorious Nazi war criminal. Bascomb first published an adult book titled *Hunting Eichmann*, but this is much more than a young adult adaptation. Bascomb created the perfect balance between history and suspense when reworking his account for a teen audience.

NEXT READS

Every Falling Star: The True Story of How I Survived and Escaped North Korea, by Sungju Lee and Susan McClelland

In a narrative suitable for younger teens and compelling enough for older ones, readers are invited into a society closed to outsiders: communist North Korea. Lee was born in the capital of Pyongyang, the son of a respected member of the military. His family lived there quite comfortably until his father lost favor after a regime change, and they were forced to move to a northern town. Then came the deadly famine that gripped North Korea in the mid-2000s. After his parents disappeared one by one while out searching for food, Lee ended up homeless, fighting for survival, the leader of a gang of kids stealing to eat. Eventually he escaped the country. Lee's story combines a harrowing survival tale with an unprecedented look inside a society ruled by terror and propaganda.

Into the Wild, by Jon Krakauer (BBYA 1997)

At age twenty-four, Chris McCandless hitchhiked into the Alaskan wilderness without provisions or a map, determined to live a life of isolated asceticism far from civilization. Four months later his body was found. Krakauer follows his own fascination with McCandless and his fate into a very personal investigation. He examines McCandless's motivations, his idealism, clues from the family he left behind, and the cross-country odyssey that preceded his death. Teens identify with McCandless's yearning for independence and adventure, for a different kind of life than one delineated by society and family. They understand his risky behavior and his lack of consideration for its consequences, perhaps because they likewise believe in their own immortality. The mystery surrounding McCandless's final weeks will never be solved. It is unfathomable and endlessly worthy of examination.

The Blind Side: Evolution of a Game, by Michael Lewis (Alex 2007)

This inspiring blockbuster combines sports strategy, biography, and social justice. Lewis begins by explaining how the offensive left tackle became a crucial position in football; without one, a quarterback can be crushed mid-throw by opponents running up on his blind side. Then Lewis introduces Michael Oher, born to a drug-addicted mother of thirteen children in Memphis and, by the time he was a young teen, usually homeless. Oher was adopted by a wealthy white family. Leigh Anne Touhy took him into her family and found tutors to help him with his schoolwork at Briarcrest Christian School, where his natural athletic talent came to the attention of the football coach. Oher was born to be a left tackle, and college recruiters flocked to his games. Readers cannot help but get caught up in Oher's unlikely success story, which was made into an award-winning movie.

Science and Discovery

Teens are constantly exploring their world, and want to understand how it works. They are also passionate advocates for environmental issues, social justice, and personal freedom. A sense of style and a sense of humor are often used to hold young readers' attention. In the past, books like *The Hot Zone* by Richard Preston and *Freakonomics* by Steven D. Levitt and Stephen J. Dubner were hits with teens. Today, medical mysteries like *Brain on Fire* by Susannah Cahalan or Rob Rufus's battle with cancer in *Die Young with Me* hit the sweet spot by incorporating memoirs into their narratives.

CORE TITLE

Eyes Wide Open: Going Behind the Environmental Headlines,
by Paul Fleischman

> Fleischman talks straight to teen readers about the environment, not only about how they can affect change on a local level, but also about the intersection of science, politics, and business, and why it is so hard to enact the changes needed to help our planet survive. This book strikes an ideal tone between telling it like it is, getting to the bottom of the issues, and working as a source book for where to learn more about each topic. The chapters on vested interests, front groups, and why even democracy itself can be harmful to the planet are eye-openers. The book's back matter begins with "How to Weigh Information" and could not be more relevant, as it walks readers through "Avoiding Being Fooled." With pages full of black-and-white photographs and sidebars, the book could have been too busy, but it somehow manages to be both attention-grabbing and serious. It also has a connected

website that is continuously updated with resources, news, and blog posts by the author.

NEXT READS

Fatal Fever: Tracking Down Typhoid Mary, by Gail Jarrow

Jarrow presents the facts about Typhoid Mary in a true crime, tabloid-style narrative, combining gruesome symptoms and historical mystery. It began with a 1903 outbreak at Cornell College, where typhoid expert George Sopher made his name by insisting on better sanitation, but not before twenty-nine students had died. In 1906, typhoid fever struck the daughter of a wealthy banker. Sopher was hired to investigate the cause. He pinpointed a young woman who worked for the family as a cook, Mary Mallon. Mallon was furious! She had never felt ill, and didn't believe that she carried typhoid. But she did indeed carry the bacteria that cause the disease. Because she refused to stop working as a cook, city officials were forced to quarantine her on an island in New York City's East River. Mallon's case caused an uproar, weighing individual rights against the public welfare.

Blink: The Power of Thinking without Thinking, by Malcolm Gladwell

Psychology is fascinating to many teens, and Gladwell's books, full of real-world examples, are go-to choices for them. Gladwell brings diverse subjects into his books about how the world, and the mind, work. *Blink* is about decision-making and intuition. Gladwell explains that decisions are governed by conscious strategy and by the adaptive unconscious (strategies that happen below the surface of consciousness). He argues that quick and instinctive actions can be as good as conscious and logical ones. His examples (from fields as disparate as art forgery, election polling, and marriage counseling) demonstrate the effectiveness of "fast and frugal" decisions, as well as their fallibility. He takes his theory further and claims that we can train ourselves to make snap judgments that are both educated and controlled. Gladwell's writing is good storytelling that gets teens thinking—and feeling smart about decision-making.

Gulp: Adventures on the Alimentary Canal, by Mary Roach

It's almost impossible to choose among Roach's irreverent and wonderfully informative books of scientific investigative journalism. While she is still best known for *Stiff: The Curious Lives of Human Cadavers, Gulp* prevails because teens are, in general, obsessed with food and eating. Readers learn about human taste testers who help create new pet foods, the phenomenon of extreme chewing, the science of food-eating contests, and the reason why crispy foods are so appealing. With her trademark glee, Roach addresses taboo subjects such as drug mules, how imprisoned convicts smuggle contraband, and the flammability of flatulence. She relishes the opportunity to go to the most gross-out extremes in her research, and she has a knack for interviewing scientists who are incredible characters. Roach's conversational writing style, especially her incorporation of clever, punning one-liners, particularly within the footnotes, is tailor-made for teen readers.

Browsing Nonfiction

In this section, we look at the type of book that teens might flip through as they sit around the library killing time, half socializing, half studying, reading aloud a funny quip, or gasping over a surprising photograph. These books are sought more for pure entertainment or quick learning than for deep immersion in a story. These include how-to books about everything from cars to hairstyles to specific crafts, as well as books of lists or sports figures, art books, cookbooks, and visual dictionaries. Magazines fit into this collection, as does the coloring book trend.

CORE TITLE

Humans of New York: Stories, by Brandon Stanton (Alex 2016)

In the vein of the 2005 phenomenon *PostSecret,* Stanton gives his readers a peek into the lives of people around them. Without staging or preparation, Stanton approaches people on the streets of New York City and they become his willing, candid subjects. And given the incredible diversity of that city, the possibilities are endless. In this book, each subject is represented by a sentence or short paragraph, accompanied by a photograph. This is the second *Humans of New York* book from Stanton, whose photography blog of the same name (or HONY, as he calls it) launched in 2010 and now has millions of followers worldwide. While teens may keep up with HONY on social media, this book is still a great browse for how much of the world it opens up and how much empathy it encourages, in such a perfectly simple manner. In recent years, Stanton has traveled the world and created special series on groups ranging from refugees to cancer patients. He shines a light on how much people have in common with each other around the world.

NEXT READS

Hamilton: The Revolution, by Lin-Manuel Miranda and
Jeremy McCarter

Fandoms hit teens hard, and the hit musical *Hamilton* is a perfect example. The subtitle of this delicious book says it all: "Being the complete libretto of the Broadway musical, with a true account of its creation, and concise remarks on hip-hop, the power of stories, and the new America." The complete lyrics for each song in the musical are preceded by an essay about its creation, hidden meanings, purpose, and musical inspirations. The lyrics are annotated with notes explaining what Miranda was trying to communicate, or why a certain phrase turned out the way it did. There are photographs, many full spreads in color, some smaller in black and white, of the actors on and off stage, as well as stories about particular moments in the show's history, such as the afternoon President Obama attended. The audiobook is also highly entertaining.

Atlas Obscura: An Explorer's Guide to the World's Hidden Wonders,
by Joshua Foer, Dylan Thuras, and Ella Morton

This quirky guide to unusual sights around the world began as a website that launched in 2009. Its creators wish to inspire wonder, and they invite their online readers to post their own finds, too. Many of the most intriguing sights are included here, organized by area of the world. Each attraction is described in two or three short paragraphs, and most include a color photo, contact information, and brief advice on how to visit it. The sights encompass both the natural and man-made, including museums, archives, temples, parks, cultural traditions, archeological finds, ruins, and unusual tourist attractions. Many highlight cultures that are changing or disappearing due to war or environmental upheaval. Teens with wanderlust, geography addicts, and those fascinated by weird or secret places are ideal readers of this book.

Steal Like an Artist, by Austin Kleon

In a convivial tone that conveys the thrill of pursuing a creative passion, Kleon offers engaging, inspiring, and practical advice on becoming a successful artist, advice that applies well beyond artistic pursuits. Kleon begins with the premise that "nothing is original," and he encourages readers to embrace influences. He does not advocate plagiarism or direct copying; he makes a clear distinction between transformation or emulation and mere imitation. Studying what you love in great depth will reveal the ideas behind the art, the thought processes behind the work. Kleon encourages artists to go ahead and create, not to wait to become an expert in their field of interest. Quotes by artists from Jay-Z to Picasso are scattered throughout. The book's small size and unusual shape, along with its quirky charts, drawings, lists, and photographs, make it appealing to teens.

Expanding Readers' Horizons into the Whole Collection

This list of true stories in film and television is a mixture of the most popular and most recommended ones, with the addition of one podcast that should not be missed.

Movies

The Central Park Five

Five innocent African American boys (ages 14–16) were persuaded to confess to a crime they didn't commit.

Fed Up

Sugar and the obesity epidemic.

Food, Inc.

For teens concerned about their food and where it comes from, this is still a good option.

Girl Rising

An inspiring film about girls around the world and the injustices they endure as they fight for access to education.

Hoop Dreams

Two Chicago high school students hope to play college basketball and go pro.

Most Valuable Players

High school musical theater performers compete for the Freddy Awards.

A Place at the Table

Food insecurity and hunger in America, and why making changes in the system is so challenging.

Television

The Bachelor/The Bachelorette
   This franchise is hugely popular with teenage girls, in particular.

I Am Jazz
   This reality show follows Jazz Jennings and her family. Her memoir *Being Jazz: My Life as a (Transgender) Teen* is also highly recommended.

Keeping Up with the Kardashians
   Fame for fame's sake is the raison d'être of this hugely popular reality show and its spin-offs, which follow members of the Kardashian and Jenner families.

Love and Hip Hop
   This series reveals the lives, loves, and work of hip-hop artists in different parts of the country.

MasterChef Junior
   Competitive cooking show featuring chefs between the ages of 8 and 13.

The Voice
   The dream of becoming a pop star is alive and well, as evidenced by this entertaining singing competition.

Podcast

Serial
   Adnan Syed was convicted of murdering his girlfriend. This reexamination plants doubts about his guilt. From the creators of NPR's *This American Life.*

Recommendations for Readers' Advisory

In working with teens who are seeking nonfiction, it is important to identify the intention of the reader. They are usually interested in a specific subject, person, or event. But they may also have a certain type of reading experience in mind, even if they do not initially articulate it. Ask questions. Include hints about appeal when making a book suggestion. In describing *The Boys Who Challenged Hitler* by Philip Hoose, point out that much of the book is comprised of Knud Pedersen's own words. This will alert memoir fans. Share that the young people were imprisoned by the Nazis to show that the stakes were high. Thriller readers will take note.

Offer nonfiction options in displays and booktalks, and avoid making assumptions about gender appeal. Kids of all ages have interests that lead them in surprising reading directions. If a book is well-written and presented in an appealing way, it will find an audience.

Keep a finger on the pulse of popular culture. Who is the next Mindy Kaling or Lena Dunham? Will the musical *Dear Evan Hansen* hit *Hamilton* status? Books by YouTube celebrities, like Dan & Phil's *The Amazing Book Is Not on Fire* and Hannah Hart's *Buffering* are trending. And fandom is huge with teens. They binge-watch their favorite shows, read and reread their favorite series, and write fanfiction. They also read about their favorite shows or about fandom itself in books like *The Fangirl's Guide to the Galaxy* or *Doctor Who: The Writer's Tale* by Russell T. Davies.

Entertainment Weekly is an excellent source of pop culture information, as is *School Library Journal*. The SLJ Teen e-mail newsletter is a great resource for staying apprised.

Keeping Up with New and Upcoming Titles

Journals

Booklist's annual Series Nonfiction issue and annual Biography issue include Top Ten lists.

VOYA Nonfiction Honor List, grades 6–8, released in August: http:// voyamagazine.com/tags/nonfiction-honor-list/

Best Books of the Year lists from *Booklist, School Library Journal, Kirkus Reviews, Publishers Weekly*, and *Horn Book.*

Awards and Lists

Alex Awards: www.ala.org/yalsa/alex-awards
This annual list of ten adult books with appeal to young adults usually includes at least one nonfiction title, and the official nomination list has more.

Boston Globe-Horn Book Awards: www.hbook.com/ boston-globe-horn-book-awards
Includes a nonfiction category.

Robert F. Sibert Informational Book Medal (ALSC): www.ala.org/alsc/
awardsgrants/bookmedia/sibertmedal/sibertpast/sibert medalpast

> Awarded annually to the author(s) and illustrator(s) of the most dis-
> tinguished informational book published in the United States in
> English during the preceding year for ages birth to fourteen.

SB&F Prize for Excellence in Science Books (AAAS): https://www
.aaas.org/page/aaassubaru-sbf-prize-excellence-science-books-about

> Includes children's, middle grade, young adult, and hands-on categories.
> 2018 winners: https://www.aaas.org/news/2018-aaassubaru-children
> -s-science-book-prize-winners-announced.

YALSA Award for Excellence in Nonfiction for Young Adults:
www.ala.org/yalsa/nonfiction

> Honors the best nonfiction book published for young adults (ages
> 12–18). Includes a vetted nominations list, which is invaluable for col-
> lection development.

YALSA Quick Picks for Reluctant Young Adult Readers: Through
2018: www.ala.org/yalsa/quick-picks-reluctant-young-adult-readers

> Beginning 2017, to be accessed through YALSA's blog, The Hub: www
> .yalsa.ala.org/thehub/

> The annual nonfiction list is the perfect place to find browsing nonfic-
> tion and, obviously, nonfiction with appeal to reluctant teen readers.

Print Resources

Fraser, Betsy. *Reality Rules! A Guide to Teen Nonfiction Reading Interests.*
Santa Barbara, CA: Libraries Unlimited, 2008.

––––––. *Reality Rules II: A Guide to Teen Nonfiction Reading Interests.* Santa
Barbara, CA: Libraries Unlimited, 2012.

Moyer, Jessica, ed. *Crossover Readers' Advisory: Maximize Your Collection
to Meet Reader Satisfaction.* Santa Barbara, CA: Libraries Unlimited,
2017.

Wyatt, Neal. *The Readers' Advisory Guide to Nonfiction.* Chicago: American
Library Association, 2007.

NOTES

1. Neal Wyatt, *The Readers' Advisory Guide to Nonfiction* (Chicago: American Library
   Association, 2007), 2.
2. Ibid, 1.

Index

CPSIA information can be obtained
at www.ICGtesting.com
Printed in the USA
LVHW051338261118
598271LV00008B/543/P